FURTHER ACCLA THE FERMENTAT

We live in a world where people choose to be defined by their outer skin and hide their true essence. The most courageous among us are willing to move beyond the trappings of position and show us another way…Arsenio is one of these. His serenades from the heart transport us, lifting us up to heights we have yet to explore. At the same time, his words take us within, gently persuading, nudging us to discover once more, what we've always known…that we are one. This is Arsenio's gift: he gives us back Ourselves..

–Sheryl Leach, *creator of Barney*

"Carefully these poems draw us into their momentum toward transcendence…they are at once cosmic and comic, transparent and knowing, humble and thrilling. Rodriguez's The Fermentation of Light is filled with an irresistible hopeful imperative "let's make eternity happen", and line by line, poem by poem, he does."

–David Gonzalez, *storyteller/musician/poet*

This book is a miracle, a symphony of psalms, a beacon of inner light. Not only the brilliance, beauty, profound wisdom and audacious wit of these poems render them unforgettable, it is the intensity of their inspiration which takes our breath away—the magnitude of their loving soul. Daring and inexorable in its sweep, "The Fermentation of Light" is intoxicating and unutterably moving. The poetry is at once astonishing and mesmerizing, poignant and exquisite, a pulsing symphonic utterance deeply empathic to human suffering, yet exuberant with hope and joy. Impassioned and ennobled, luscious and visionary. Arsenio glimpses the cosmic fire, weeps with songs of compassion, and laughs with the Immortals.' A treasure.

–Lorin Hollander, *pianist*

Kyoko

THE FERMENTATION OF LIGHT

THE FERMENTATION OF LIGHT

ARSENIO RODRIGUEZ

Printed in the United States of America

Set in Cantoria and Mrs. Eaves.

Cover illustration "Camino de Luz" by Olga Signoret
Design by Mónica Miranda

This book is dedicated to Meher Baba whose ancient story of love opened my heart. I had the fortune to meet and exchange His embraces echoing in the arms of his true lovers. Those who accompanied the Beloved this turn, made me see myself in them, see the beauty of the human heart. Their voices have been imprinted in me forever. Now as I continue to unfold towards the Ocean foretold, I have a Friend in my heart, always. Always...

ACKNOWLEDGEMENTS

Many people have contributed to make this book possible. Most of them are characters reflected in the sentiments and imagery used in this poetic prose that journals my passage through life. My mother Lolita for teaching me the art of reflection, my sister Olga for her kindness of forever, and her art piece "Camino de Luz" which adorns the cover of this book. My wife Julie and my children, Marimer, Illya, Merwan and Meheradi, for their patience and love in putting up with my absence of mind all these years, as I went on these lonely fishing journeys for poetry and meaning (that are still going on!). My friends Pedro Miranda (Pochi) and Marcos Ramirez, who have listened patiently to these lines in nights of red wine.

My deep friends from the Alliance of a New Humanity with whom I have shared on different occasions some of these verses and in whose heart reactions, I found encouragement to continue writing, as I realized that if the heart was being shared, I was establishing a communication with them that went beyond just words. There are so many to name, but here are a few: Michael Fiur, Jeff Dunn, Alice Savic, Brenda Isaac, Valerie Jackson, Roberto Savio, Cherian Eapen, Bruce Schearer, Lorin and Tara Hollander, Nandita Das, David Gonzalez, Fred Johnson, Laurie Meadoff, Paul Taylor, Dale Colton and Michael Karlin. I have never in such a short period of time met such a diverse and inspired group of people, they all have enriched my passing by.

I want to thank specially my friend Deepak Chopra, for his encouragement, his invitation for me to publish some of these poems in his Intent Blog, and the beautiful foreword. I thank him for his incredible energy at the service of the manifestation of love and consciousness that has earned my respect and admiration. For indeed this "man in black" is doing an amazing work in calling the attention of so many to the important things in life: inner poise, unity consciousness, Love, joy, and forgiveness.

I wish to thank Howard Rosenfeld and Sheryl Leach for surprising me in December 2005 with a great love-gift, a leather bound compilation of my poems, "Cantos". That engendered the vision of what today has become the Fermentation of Life.

A special thanks to my dear friend and colleague Mabel Lassalle, who through her "velvet hammer" persistence, has been insisting non-stop that I publish my poetry. You can rest now Mabel. The deed is done.

I wish to thank Summer Turner for her heartfelt edits and recommendations, Danny Ladinsky for his encouragement, Mónica Miranda for her skills in book and cover design.

Finally thanks to all who have read and who will read these pages. Thanks for accompanying me a moment or two in these reflections about our passage. I am humbled by your sharing.

CONTENTS

FOREWORD

Ever since I was a child I was drawn to poetry. My grandmother would recite to me sacred verses from the mythic traditions of India where gods and goddesses frolicked in celestial playgrounds. Mystery, magic, wonder and enchantment expressed in verse became the raw materials of my imagination. Later in my childhood I was introduced to the poems of Kabir, Rumi, and Tagore who through rhythm and rhyme brought me a sacred world that I knew existed and was real, and yet beyond my reach in the world of everyday reality. It was nonetheless, a world that my soul yearned for…the agony of wishing and not finding.

As I grew up I came across the poems of Emily Dickinson, D.H. Lawrence, Byron, Shelley, Coleridge, Blake, Shakespeare, Chaucer, and Alfred, Lord Tennyson. I began to understand the meaning and effect of onomatopoeia, where the sounds echoes the sense and where just the recitation of songs, ballads and poems can lift you out of everyday existence, transporting you to higher states of awareness.

Even to day, if I close my eyes to hear the exquisite verse of Tennyson's "Idylls of the King" I can see on the screen my consciousness and hear through the stereophonic sound system of my imagination… the clash of armies on the Isle of Avalon. I can sense the crunch of ice as the armored heels of King Arthur and his brave, wounded knights trudge across the snowy fields of England.

Look at the following words and see for yourself how your physiology reacts to the nostalgia of a bygone era.

> Dry clashed his harness in the icy caves,
> and the bare black cliff clang round him
> as he based on his fee on juts of slippery crag
> that rang sharp, smitten with the dint of armed
> heels…and on the sudden lo — the level lake and the
> long glories of the winter moon.

Even now, as I read these lines I am taken inexplicably to a world that I've only experienced in the imagination, but always longed to know.

Poetry is — in the words of T.S. Eliot — a "raid on the inarticulate." This is because poetry, like meditation, allows us to slip into the gap between thoughts and get in touch with the karmic software of our souls. Here are insights and epiphanies, revelations and a world of enchantment, such as we have never dreamed of in our ordinary waking state of consciousness.

The following selection of poems are an offering from the heart of Arsenio Rodriquez. I have known Arsenio for many years. He has a background as a consultant of various organizations and has held responsible and key positions at the World Bank as well as the United Nations. Most recently Arsenio has been the Secretary General for Alliance for a New Humanity. He has spearheaded as organized the annual Human Forum for five years. The Alliance for a New Humanity is committed to creating a critical mass, consciousness in the world for personal and planetary transformation.

Although I have known Arsenio in all of these roles, when I think of him, most often, I think of him as a poet. The poems contained in this beautiful volume are full of seeking, longing, sensitivity, vulnerability, pain, anguish, joy, love, and the intoxication of divine ecstasy. They are the flavors through which the human heart expresses itself as it searches for unity consciousness. As I have read them, a couplet, a stanza there or just a single line catches my attention and gives me a moment of delightful revelation. It is my hope that as you read these verses you will also have the same experience.

DEEPAK CHOPRA

INTRODUCTION

Ever since I can remember I have been mesmerized by the incredible phenomenon of being alive and aware. The magic of it all. Throughout my youth, I was desperately searching for the meaning of this ephemeral beauty that bloomed and withered in a short span of time, and that seemed to be unevenly distributed in terms of peoples opportunities for joy and choice. I was concerned about how transient and how unfair everything was. Concepts were passed on to me in surrounding culture and religion, but they were surface deep, I remained unconvinced, and demanded a realization based on something other than peoples dogmas and interpretations. I had to find my own truth.

The feminine has always played a great role in the shaping my life. From my mother who was a beacon of soul, my first loves, my wife, my sister. They all have amazed me for their strength of giving, their depth of feeling, and their joy of living, in spite of all the challenges they had to face in a world designed by men's child games. Woman of holy water, "Mujer de agua bendita" the poem that opens this diary refers to this deep rooted admiration and love for the feminine.

Later in life I met a woman in India, Mehera Irani, chief disciple of Meher Baba, who for me represented the essence of femininity. I met her from afar, never even shook hands with her or embraced her, yet she glanced into my eyes, she smiled, and she opened up inner wells of pure water that soothed me. Through her eyes I confirmed the beauty and transcendence of perennial womanhood. She opened recesses inside where my own femininity lived. Because of her I was aware that I could sing. That is when poetry started to coalesce inside.

In the early eightie's, as I was doing some business travel in Europe, I came across in a train with a young girl. She must have been in her early twenty's or late teens. By her complexion she looked Latin, although we never spoke. She was carrying a large backpack and on it I saw her name written: Angeles. Her eyes crossed mine, so different we were,

I was a mature man in a business suit doing important things, she was a girl with fire of discovery in her black eyes, devouring the world. Somehow she made a deep impression in me. Somehow I felt then we are all backpacking, we are all journeying through this world from birth to death, devouring the world to understand ourselves. I took out a pen and wrote some lines in verse inspired by those seeking eyes. She prompted the poetry to come out.

I do not know what happened to Angeles. Maybe in another turn of the wheel we shall meet again. Maybe she had a wonderful time in Europe and integrated her experiences, recording them in her life, making her by now a seasoned traveler, a great woman, a mother, a lover, a poet, a writer.

That day I also became a backpacker in disguise. I took notes of every corner I passed, of every situation encountered, every inner mood, every twist in a relationship with the so many I met. My backpack became full to the brim with feelings of all sorts.

I recently sat down and opened it up and all these images and words flowed like a story told by a grandmother. The only hope I have now, is that you bypass form, when you are reading these notes of a backpack journey. Just sit down with me, and savor the nooks and corners of place and soul they describe, see if they match your own backpacks. If one or two of my lines do that for you, then this book would be meaningful. It would have fermented light into love.

Wholeheartedly,
Arsenio

WOMAN OF HOLY WATER; THE FEMININE FERMENT

WOMAN OF HOLY WATER

Wing flutter of delicate butterflies
in random flight.
Wing-touch in subtle space,
careening formations absolutely divine.

Then we fly down somewhere, guided by secrets.
Those mysteries, those hints sublime,
lovingly lurking behind every pebble
and beetle of this rock garden:
suddenly everything blooms in green and pink.

I can see your heart beating,
flannelled in feminine,
nourishing
sources of water that I cannot reach.

Aquifers of holy woman water
I know lie deep within me, and I yearn to drain,
to flood this arid parched terrain
of thinking that defines.

You appear, like a mariposa in the distant clouds,
your woman-expressed soul helping me,
naturally,
as feminine does,
to understand and transform my longing to dream.

To renew my dreams.

HER NAME WAS MEHERA

She stopped me one night in the middle of nowhere
under a full moon and ancient tunes,
in a faraway land of pilgrims overjoyed
for having had the company of the One they loved.

She said — with eyes of Universe and rose —
"There are three stories I must tell before you go."
And my soul forgot the stories but never her voice,
nor the meaning of all that they contained.

So now I just want to tell her,
as she must have been crowned Queen of all creation
because she loved so purely,
that I remember her verse as she told me those heart stories
with the voice of the Ancient One on her lips.

The night melted in me, the stars collapsed to the ground
and became a carpet for your feet so tender,
as I walked beside you to our final adios.

Now, I just wander in this city without stories or eyes,
making an effort to remember the meaning and the rhymes.
What can I say, about love divine?

I melted always on her porch and in her garden,
I didn't want to be anywhere but there,
look at her in adoration, catch her glances and smiles,
flying like angels in my direction?

Just one last point.
I have never doubted the secret that she whispered in my heart,

and although I cannot remember it,
It has bloomed in an invisible Garden
that all can see, except me.

AN ETERNAL DATE

Words are blunt chisels,
to sculpt feelings of the heart

That sensation of warmth
That angst in your chest,
The longing of your spirit
That soothing embrace
The glory of the encounter.

They lie beyond the reach
Of descriptive sounds,
or discrete contents
in sentence, verse and dictums

What one feels can only be shared
from within, among those
who know what they are not.

It is a song that spills
A wordless poem
A Silence
A caress
A glance
A kiss

Come, let's sit together now,
in this moment of universe,
between falling waters
and brewing torments.

Let's only be breeze
aside from thoughts
just be here in us.

Everything stops in this music
in this rhythm of silences shared.

This exquisite filigree has been engraved
through million millenniums
It shapes our vantage points
defined in our acknowledged forms

It is not a cosmic coincidence
that we now sit glancing at each other.
this is after all a designer's universe

There is a most particular song
that has never been sung.
It can only be played entre nous
In a duet of souls seasoned
by a long journey of two.

Let's consecrate in celebration
this universal art exhibit,
and savor this moment of rest
now that the train has rest-stopped
and just let go in each other
without purpose or meaning

Let's become one in a glance,
melt our bodies in amalgam
in the crucible of our presence.
Revert our colors in the prism

so only light as light shines
without hue.

Lets embrace in an embrace
to confirm and marvel
at the serene awe of life.
Let's make eternity happen!

We must mark our agendas
for the next encounter
at the next rest station.
To renew our vows
to celebrate this incredible story

Of love

MELLOW MOMENTS

Consciousness meanders everywhere,
like an overflowing river.
Absorbing every drop of light and dark,
in outsides and insides woven, as life.

Sometimes it rushes to conclusions
and beats in thought-filled temples
with rhythms of certainty

Other occasions it lingers,
mellow in watery shallow ponds,
where even reflections are quiet

It filters through inaccessible moods
in woods of paralyzed enchantment.

Eyes look then, but do not see, except boundaries.
Senses are dull in an overwhelming everything
Nothing is queried, all goes along.

Yet, accumulated heartaches manifest in bundles,
and footfall stumbles in the blinding presence
that surrounds all sounds, in a merciless quietude.

Words rumble in agony of not being heard
and birds sing as always, without much ado,
in a marvelously silent explosion of color and musts,
that envelops the totality of perception
in mellow moments with you.

A BLESSING

I wish music fills your life spaces. That most subtle angels, take your hands and walk you over through the enchanted cosmic forests of existence. I wish the Ocean spills in your eyes and replenishes all your moments with depth and tenderness. For starlight to melt in sidereal rains and flood every secret orbital of your body and its impossible nexus with your soul, to provoke an eternal smile in your flowering lip gardens.

I wish that universes contract, and pose themselves like seagulls in your heart, expanding it with all the feelings and turmoil of life, making it explode like a volcano in your bosom of mother, and make you aware of your arms of father.

I wish all colors are woven in a magic carpet of legend, so your beautiful feet, that have trodden for ages, now paint masterpieces as they serenely walk the Earth again.

I wish my words reflect my heart as I remember you, in this day of forever that started never. In that mystery of majestic Being, in those moments of light and song, so ancient that can only be remembered as what has not yet been. This love tapestry, sown by long fingers of yesterday, by sages with flowing beards of wisdom, by fires and hungers of lust and solitude, by so many journeys together in bygone times.

Pilgrims we are linked in this never ending search, hand in hand advancing silently, only our love lighting the horizon. So many lives, so many roles, so many kisses exchanged, so many children conceived within our wombs, so much synchrony of mind.

I wish one day, forgiveness flourishes in the treasures you hold inside, and spreads through your longing eyes to escape in embraces so tender, that can be heard in millions voices, like the enchanted melodies that have accompanied us all through millennia. That we can still, in spite of the veil of circumstance, rise like the dead touched by Love, and dance in gratitude with the universe in infinite gyres of joy. That we can dream our dreams.

I wish to give you a kiss of Light that melts inside your soul, so that you can feel this immense love, this morning of mornings, this symphony of symphonies that invades my soul, whenever I remember you.

SEEKING YOUR WOMB

Where are you apparition?
Where are your smiles of new mornings
and eyes of yesterday's suspicions?

What new uncertainties are you weaving with postures
of female?
Why do you leave me, and hide behind curtains drawn,
when this play has only begun?

I can see you still, sweetly and sensuously revealed
apple bites in your hands and wild songs in your hair.

Every cell of mine holds tight for integrity,
every time I think of you

I miss you these nights of incomplete bedcovers
as my bones are exposed to cold shudders.

I dream about you
in tempests of assaulting images,
during endless nocturnal battles,
I end up exhausted, drained.

My arms torn from waving and embracing chimeras.
My loins in an unrequited fire of searching in vain,
for the river basin of your formless body
for your lipless kisses.

Like a stripping flower
I scatter myself in the inner winds
and my seeds spread throughout the universe.

Seeking your Womb.

A SPECIAL RENDEZVOUS

This night of absolute darkness,
sacred chants and moaning forms,
seek each other passionately
amongst the shadows.

I dream of you in Heaven and Earth

Your image emerges in mystery,
like a fragrance, like a whisper.
It draws itself in my thoughts,
elongates in my silence.

Where are you now?
Sweetly wayfaring towards our encounter?
What latitudes is your arrow body crossing,
as it flashes through the sky,
towards that ancient point of departure,
where all voices and moments were born?

To that place, where we remember without memory,
this journey in masquerade of centuries.

In this absolute night of remembrance
I hear you in my heart.
The melody of your kisses,
is fresh in my breath.

Today, in renewed migration towards your arms
I feel the world spinning
and subtle premonitions turn clouds into visions.

Nothing is more defined now
than your presence in my life.
The sacred urns of my soul
are filled with unknown memories of you.

We fly diverse routes towards our rendezvous

Unknowingly

Vast ocean shores of infinity
smiles in lips, caresses in tenderness.
To fulfill our yearnings.

A SINGLE EMBRACE OF MOTHER

Concepts are spoken and written, about everything.
in endless chit chat of mind asserting.

Meantime one witnesses the changing soul seasons:
nostalgia and joy, awe and sublimity, presence, tenderness,
passion and observance and all their shades and shadows.

They squeeze by, like silent tectonic plates
shaping the horizons of life,
notwithstanding the hubris of intellect and mind.

Words have reached the brim, books and lectures
have saturated my noosphere.
They have attained their purpose in this adventure,
leading me to conclude with absolute conviction
that all concepts together don't compare with the revelation
that is present in a single embrace of mother.

ANTICIPATED SPRING

All this hiding, my dear, all this seeking,
it runs so old, so deep, it jumps spaces and times.

That we now fly like homing pigeons
to each others' nests is no surprise.

Together we have won battles and lost families,
we have conquered hearts and betrayed ourselves,
and we have lied and sacrificed.

We hold roses and thorns in every hand,
poems, words of love, songs sublime.

We hum them, as we traverse these fields of memory,
as we weave this nakedness that uncovers and hurts like raw skin,
as we howl moons down to bathe us in golden light of promised lands.

Springtime is seasonal, we know,
but seasons grow ancient
and accumulate and bloom in cycles of everlasting,
where layers of garden become so thick
that every breath is a flower offered in love
and every tear is a crystalline fountain of joy anticipated.

The springtime of spring is dawning;
let's embrace as we bloom in its gardens tilled in Silence.

All this dryness will pass soon.
All these winds will calm down.

THIS QUIETUDE OF MOON

This quietude of moon forebodes ancient runes of enchantment.
The sphere shines, magically suspended in our perception,
showering a cool, soothing light that ferments like wine in the mind,
and displaces convention.

Howls are being heard in caverns below,
as creatures of instinct and energy,
accumulated throughout evolution,
react to primeval moon calls.

Alchemies of wild secret formulas
cascade in the turbulence of unforeseen consequences;
fragrances of touch are bubbling up from subterranean spaces,
caressing the skin from within,
affecting its tone with a sensation of presence.

What nocturnal rhythms are being played by the long moon fingers,
as they bounce and illumine those feminine hills at dusk?

Light-inebriated melodies are inviting kisses in serenity,
effervescing from deep pools of ancient memory,
entangled particles are racing through the heavens,
dissolving in the wisdom of pause
in a mystical primordial hunger of bodies and feeling.

There is a nakedness that scares prudence and custom
as latent lovers in rose blooms garden together their Earth,
imbibing ancient moon orders, like nocturnal florescence.

Moonbeams are serenely disturbing peace of mind,
creating a impression of two who are One,
inducing a transparent glow
that encompasses all dimensions of form and invisibility.

Urging an embrace of forever.

FOREVER KISSES

I want to have wakeful dreams
that rhyme and spill,

that silently intertwine between us
and reach
things not happened yet.

Spirit hands, limbs made of wind,
would dissolve the distance.

Nested in your vortex
I will cuddle up.

The galaxies expanding in caresses,
every atom will become a kiss.

Universes are entanglements of bodies.

All seeking has stopped in finding you,
All words swallowed.

I dreamed you awake.
In an everlasting morning.

Night stars witnessed this love,
forever kisses exploded suddenly;
and inevitably we became.

ATLANTIC OCEAN OF LIGHT

Our elongated arms were so extended
that they disconnected from the main.

The Atlantic Ocean, wept out of our eyes,
had taken us by surprise
as the sunset colored everything
in tropical pastels of light.

We walked like pilgrims for ages,
reviving evolution and history,
pacing that small shore at dusk.

We shed tears as we discovered our secrets
and forgave our trespasses,
as we understood about the meek, and the beatitudes,
in our own flesh and experience.
Our sandaled feet treading paths of antiquity.

Light surrounded everything;
your face was peeking out from a full moon
as inequities paraded in harmony before our gaze.

Movement was a glowing globe
floating in a sea of luminosity.

For hours that seemed ages,
we poured out our hearts to each other
and cried in awe at the discovery of our ancient walk.
Smiles of music resounded in our fused mental bodies,
and the face of the Beloved shone.

And we knew then why He loved.

Every facet, every contrast, every pain, every joy,
no matter how scandalous or horrid,
how blissful or ecstatic, was ours, ours alone.
It was all part of the same score,
that same melody inundating all.

We died and saw our spirits,
in synchronistic reverie,
drowned in the Atlantic Ocean of Light.

That day, that wonderful sunset by the beach
with ancient castles and clouds in rose,
so beautifully arranged for you and me.

HAVEN'T YOU AT ALL NOTICED?

Long arms to embrace you several times around I wish I had.
To keep you with me and pull you from afar.

I am sand lying naked by the shore untouched by waves.
You are a wave that comes so near,
but when I prepare for your wet kiss,
you turn back and merge in the immense Ocean.

This hunger for you has been growing;
it is a burning, a dark night, a vacuum,
a shout in desperation.

I have searched under all covers; savagely I have torn so many clothes,
looking for your loveliness.
I have tried so many formulas and enchantments and magic potions,
so many seductive words and glances.
I have flirted with you — haven't you at all noticed?

All I get is either silence or conversations about something else.
You know what I want and need;
you know this yearning that makes me so fragile and vulnerable and prey
to so many dangerous creatures that, like chameleons,
dress up as you and leave my mouth hurting
with fraudulent kisses.

I yearn so long and wide that no one knows
that I have died.
They even think I can give them life,

only you and I are fully aware that until you love me
I will not be whole or useful to anybody.

So please, my dear, stop being so prudish and elusive and come to my arms and make me yours.

After all, I already am.

INEVITABLE LOVE

In this darkness of uncertainty I love you
In this planetary acceleration I dream of you
In this spatial distance I await for you

Who are these adventurous and mischievous spirits of ours,
that transcending all possibility and civility,
ignoring time's irreversibility,
come to dance, dance again, in this carnival?

And they let go, as they seek and surrender to each other.

Yet not knowing

In a plot, long forgotten by accountants
while well known by poets,
they listen to each other, they touch,
they gaze, they wait upon one another,
they become one, then they die.

Not knowing why.

YET I MISS YOU

My arms reach out for your essence,
and I think of you in the path of stars,
remembering the ancient times of our encounters,
when your caresses lightened up my captivity.

My mind is lost in circumstance,
in those streets and gardens of nowhere,
that we walked together.

I long being with you.
Even without knowing
if you will be present in the embrace.
Even if all is just a mirage born of loneliness.

Inevitably, I miss you

FALLOPIAN TUBES

Take a break, as you flutter eyes and wings
so you can see and soar.
Multitudes surround you with animosities,
intent, demands, praise and complaints.

Universes of verses, words of swords
have been written in song.
The periscope eyes,
are looking, name-dropping,
comparing, judging, laughing.

Just take a little break,
as the curtains now fall between acts.
Relax my sister.

Stretch your legs, walk about ,
go outside into the astral alley,
have a smoke or breathe some fresh air,
just freshen-up and come back with dignity
to meet your destiny.

It is just a role after all, and you know it,
and who knows, maybe you will strike it big,
and become a celebrity for a while.

Think about when you were there
in a post-uterine corner
Incomplete

Waiting for the flagellate legions masculine
to die by the millions in your porch
till one could sing.

My sister life, so vast are you
that you encompass all possibility of singing.
How come you are not in bliss and
spaced out in self contemplation?

Just think, as you are caught up
listening to so many voices.
Trying, to sail seas of opinions
and to swim with or against current thinking.

Your role is sound,
whether you, are happy or not with the presentation.
In spite of the flavors of sweet applause,
or the bitterness of insulting jeers,
coming from your imagined audience.

Let go sister life,
the curtains will fall anytime now, rest assured.
So go back in the alley
for a smoke and some time.

To wait for the next function, the next act,
to tumble down again through Fallopian slides
to find your completion,
and recombine again, in yet another role.

You will have another voice, another opinion,
until you get tired of judging yourself in others,
and start singing under all conditions.

Until you discover the ancient streams of life
that vibrate in you and all.

So, go back with a smile to the universal theater
and play your story like never before,
knowing is endless and sacred,
and the audience too.

That your story is born
to make love happen, in me and you.

THIS ANCIENT MELODY AWAKENING US ALL

Tonight, navigating these streams of light,
I touch you remotely from this corner of the universe.

I wonder if you can feel
alongside with seeing
these binary words on your screen,

this warmness of heart that emerges when I think of you,

— as my fingers play the keyboard,
composing silent symbols of sound and thought.

My heart yearns for your presence.
It hums an intimacy;
it joys a foreboding of union;
it melts in the unison of wonder.

Somehow beyond this conduit of electrons
it reaches out
in dimensions invisible.

We embrace like lost children found.
And know there has never been any distance.

For those who are united in love know no separation.

THE CREATURE THAT GURGLES

These rhythms of life's doldrums invented by my weary mind
are shared with you, my dear,
in the context of all these anguishing perceptions of imagination within.

What can I do under these circumstances?
but to want to see your nakedness in secret,
as you look at me with practical business eyes?

I must smile.

There is a creature within me that gurgles and lights up fires
in dark watery wells
every time my daydreaming bounces against your need to categorize
these boxes of space
into classes and domains of things defined and monitored.

I wonder at all the different moods
that veil our sympathies and prevent our cascading in song.

I weep at not knowing
and yearn for that longing of flying at low altitude
through those plains of remembrance and quietude.

There serenity lies in oceans of understanding
and we can touch naked without fears of exposing
the vulnerable skins of our feelings
and the omnipotent nature of our fragility.

I sigh at the laughter that sprinkles the garden with flowers
of all colors displacing clouds in rainbows of golden rains
whenever our eyes and minds meet in harmony of being.

And we remember who we really are, my dear.

THIS NAKEDNESS SO SHY

Tonight I sigh,
inviting myself to this nakedness
so shy,

to this revelation so near
yet so far.

And you look at me askance.

I stretch my invisible arms through space
and time

to embrace you, my dear, in our pain, our joy —
in the wholeness we are.

This loneliness must rejoice into vintage wine.
How else to explain the stars in your eyes?

THIS IMMACULATE CONCEPTION

Meet me, in this mellow morning of yellow and blue,
within this space of the absolute,
as we walk among the fallen arpeggios
that rained through the night.

As our bare feet step on soft forms,
musical souls stir up like phosphorescence,
and fill the air with an intense aromatic concert
for all the subtle senses
that in our spirit body we enjoy today, my dear.

You look so lovely, with your light so radiant—
Have you been laughing asleep again?
Has your transparent heart been inundated
with cosmic longing and roses
and coziness in wall hangings and mementos?

My dear, this evolution of love and consciousness
that is reflected in us,
this moon-sun interplay of light divine,
mixed with earth and fire and all kinds of elemental particles,
are meant to provide
the adventurous essence of this cosmic promenade.

So good to have met you at these crossroads
in this Garden
that was never lost but is being created as we move along.

Let us continue our silent conversation,
as we walk these magical, enchanted fields of being,

and discover the beauty we set out to imagine,
that first moment when we conceived
this immaculate conception.

Let us joy-step ahead hand-in-hand
in this mellow morning of yellow and blue.

EXACTLY LIKE YOU

Love-Madness comes in singular explosions
that cannot be predicted,
explained or compared.

So who knows where this is coming from?
But eruptions are there;
Lava rivers are devastating pretty houses and poses.
We are dealing with fire here,
dancing on the rim of a fathomless well.

I am woozy, my skin is burning,
I have a strange sensation in my head,
a humming sound of sea that doesn't cease.

I feel new life opening collapsed veins,
red-wine nights by placid lakes.

Deep conversations held only with the eyes,
deep longings for the most sublime,
moonlit spaces in my inner worlds.

What do I feel?
Everything!
How am I feeling?
Don't you know?
Exactly like you, my dear,
Exactly like you.

YOU WILL NOW RUN AWAY FROM ME

This skin is bothering me so much,
I am going to peel myself — the whole body —
like an animal I have slain in the forest
to reveal inner layers delicately tender
and perfectly harmonized with each other.

I will then stand naked with my innards out for all to see,
my vanity gone with the hide that covered my personality...

You will see only beating hearts,
livers detoxifying, and lungs purifying energy,
eyeballs envisioning light,
and raw nerve endings sensing the weather.

All that form, that profile, those ruby lips,
the eyebrows that signaled interesting faces
I have taken away with the hunter's knife,
to reveal the fantastic agglomeration
of astonishing cells in organs organized,
laboriously glorifying creation by expressing within
their simple functions dutifully performed in profound humility,
serving the wish of God to know Himself,
to express the Love and enjoy the Beauty.

You will now run away from me,
as I approach you with my red muscles
and tendons hanging from the bones of my arms,
the mask of my face grotesquely revealed.

You will see my heart beating for you,
my entrails contracting in all manner of signals of empathy;
yet you will not see the fiction invented to give a role to that entity,
that bearer of a moment of divinity
who was supposed to praise and love the Universe
but instead became enamored of his mirror image.

Now the mirror image has vanished with the discarded skin.
And I still love you with these ragged miraculous insides and muscles;
I still love you, for my love, woman of God,
comes from the source of the form,
and is in absolute harmony with the incandescent beauty
of that moon that shines eternally from your breast.

SONGS OF FERMENTATION AND BREW

INTIMACY OF BODY

I bow humbly at the intimacy of body.

Endowed with a magnifying x-ray glass.
I could see the sacred intimacies.
Those laborious cells miraculously singing
in organismic orchestration —
in processes in synchrony.

Runaway ions crossing membranes,
nested coves of protein
allowing quiet lovemaking between molecules,
places where they couple cozily, establishing relationships
that procreate essential worlds
in that firmament of fluids, internal rivers,
synthesis and excretion.

I marveled at my now-aging joints,
how flexible were these hands
that I discovered as a baby.
When I marveled at finding that they were connected to me.

I stand in awe at the intimacy of body:

At the crisscrossing ions
creating fluxes of electrical impulses
upon which sensitivity travels,
connecting all cells and tissues.
At the secretion of fluids and
the incorporation of ingredients that nourish
this body-temple that houses the mind.

I am astonished at the inventiveness of mind
as she integrates perception —
light, sound, caresses, fragrances, and flavors.
Conceiving in space-time magnificent forms,
concepts in thought, dreams, quests,
technologies that expand the hands
and endow the senses with remote sensing.

Roller coasting through my veins,
I traveled capillary country roads,.
stopped for coffee on cellscapes,
watching the gurglings and whooshes
of ions crossing membrane borders.
I witnessed the quiet lovemaking of molecules
in cozy enzyme rooms
while trying to understand the backstage
where thoughts are assembled.

I am humbled and amazed at the multidimensionality of this temple.
I stand in awe at the intimacy of body.

YET ANOTHER INFINITE ANGLE

Amazed, truly amazed at the simultaneous complexity and simplicity of all,
I emerged from sleep unconsciousness and recovered my identity:
my place in time and space,
the web of relationships,
the cross-currents of thoughts,
memories, and desires that flash constantly
through the labyrinths of mind.

All conversations, expectations, duties, tendencies
and yearnings gathered to laugh in a merry choir of "me",
as I looked "outside" to see
the substance that nourishes and envelops everything,
ever so loyal, ever so subtle.

I can only wonder and try to capture the tender tension
between what has been and what will be,
hinging on this ephemeral and eternal Is.
It bedazzles me as I wake up and look at the misty morning
through the misty eyes of my misty soul.

With an effortless elongation of some invisible extremities,
I embrace the ineffable once again and yearn for poise.
Yet even this yearning is but a figment of this very creative imagination
bubbling from the Universe in its most immense simplicity
to experience from yet another infinite angle,
another infinite perspective, the possibilities of Being.

This misty morning, birds were remotely singing inside
of clouds fallen to the ground,
and contradictory moments were peeking
from behind the fence of the unconscious
into this show-time arena of that called me.

In the sudden Silence of the sudden morning,
suddenness arrives with its distant chains of woven moments
that shape the tapestry of everything, I feel and dream I am.

Without saying any word, name, formula or not,
or moving any movement of this substance
that seemingly embodies me,
I pronounce a song of thanks and marvel,
I fall reverently while I stand high,.
merge and yet away to continue the expected weaving,
because that particular and infinite angle of crafted unique realization
is impossibly embedded within me and needs to be.

A MAGIC ORCHESTRA

Every single moment is magic,
disguised in clothes of ordinariness.
Light shines bright through every second.

Symphonies of shared sound, as faces, round
with eternity's yearning, smile in colors,
like rainbows, when our presences interact in space-time,
overlapping their luminescence of soul journeying.

Every point is a universe created, every instant a sublime projection,
of love essence potential, painting itself in expression
as it glows and rolls every wave and drop in its imagination.

Stop, and see the shining of everything, all thoughts and words
woven in concert, as we try to pin down within our own realm
the meaning of this song profound, or escape the awe of the surround,
turning our heads sideways, hiding in sequences remembered, or
anticipated.

Now, is the only moment you can seize,
music forms are painted in the air,
by an inspired body waving butterfly arms.
The resonating stage is filled with aspirations of soul
in tune and rhythm they respond,
with heart-hands out of which
grow violins, cellos, and trombones.

Four hands move in a love of ages
across the black and white keyboard of a magic piano,
playing an audience of hearts enthralled in a moment of music.

All now are singing melodiously, longing for that kiss of knowing,
of becoming for one second awake to the reality of their oneness.

Music is lived as we reveal each other to each other,
and our galaxies merge, in sentiment and occasion.
Then universes expand in heart beats, as we meet and greet and recognize,
unconsciously, the vastness of every moment that passes by.
As we recreate each other, from vantage points that flash in the sky,
in multiple reflections and apparitions of Beauty in sound and sight.

Laughter, words of guidance, ancient maps, new frontiers, silence,
mantras and meditation, or just conversation and tales,
intimations of who we are, of our trajectories registered in diaries of passers-by.
Svelte women in Nordic goddess attire, music-people with hands divine,
women and men of all flavors and dispositions looking forward in reflection,
living each such extraordinary moments, as we witness on every second
a magic orchestration recreating worlds in imagination and sense.

IN AN EVERY DAY

Memories and feelings melted
in the footfall of searching, striding feet.
Your smile was dawning in silhouette,
knitted by the hands of the sublime.

Timeless, the golden Silence became the walk and the talk.
We succumbed to time in grains of minutes and sand
dispersed by winds of words and depths of sentiments divine.

One every day we woke up all of a sudden
in no time at all.
We saw the invisible
and talked about the unreachable

until nothing happened and we dissolved again

extraordinarily into the glorious ordinariness
that we permanently are.

And we laughed heartily;
no one heard anything anymore, but sound and words
till we became deaf to forms and norms.

bursting into stars and lilies, notwithstanding prohibition,
falling and drowning in that Ocean-Sky, wetting the dry in us.

One afternoon in an everyday, nowhere in space
Everywhere in time,

we became sublime.

CONSCIOUSNESS OF MORNING

This miracle of light and consciousness
dawned again.
Suddenly, from a no-place where my periscope was closed,
I opened my eyes to see anew.

To recognize.

First, the awareness of waking,
a sense of knowing, a moment of un-associated consciousness.

Then came body perception of limbs and sinew.
Finally, the personality I am branded with.

Looking out, I saw trees so green
extending their arms in supplicant's praise,
awed and grateful for the sun's shower of nutritious light.

Their roots sapping moisture and subterranean atoms,
in an alliance of life that gave birth to shape and function.

This glorious morning, my eyes were able to see again
integrating surrounding forms
into processes of beauty and understanding
just turning my head, as I woke up to individuality.

I stood up, defying gravity, and in a coordination of movements so complex
(it took perhaps a billion industrious cells)
I walked, marvel of marvels, displacing this form in space.

I breathed oxygen-coated energy exhaled by surrounding green forms

that synthesized sunlight in leaf, flower, fruit, and bark.
I exhaled back and gave them carbon resulting from my burning,
as I walked and breathed, thought, admired, and kissed,
so perfectly in time,
acquiring every possible experience,
like an alien on a mission on Planet Earth,

Worker bee cells in hives ordained,
laboriously enabling, through anciently coded processes
and swimming particles,
this perception, this coordinated action, this vantage point

from where I can see, touch and admire all bundles of Being
that populate this exquisite forest of forms
expressed in all possibility of imagination.

Vibrating, singing, dancing the rhythms of life
this glorious morning of space and time,

where I have met you and discovered your uniqueness,
as we intertwine our inner awe in song and appreciation —
as we love.

Today, I must kneel in secret at the blinding light
of this incredible Love
that makes all happenings possible

and laugh, in joy and gratitude
at this incredible Being we all are
that imagines this Beauty supreme
just to be, just to enable the flow

of Love.

A FEATURE PRESENTATION

Swallows fly in erratic patterns,
swirling winds of wings,
as they surge and dive against the graying sky.

Elongating in horizons, my arms try to embrace them in vain,
as my thoughts elusively turmoil themselves into moods, hurricanes,
desires, and other fluttered imaginings.

I lie down, my eyes transfixed by so many outer and inner flights,
and I wonder in serenity
at the luminescence of this everlasting presence of certainty
that silently watches these previews and feature presentations,
and envelops everything in an instant eternal.

EVEN GOD WONDERS AT BUTTERFLIES

Innumerable notions and imaginings surround me;
like characters in a novel, they define.

Anxiously, these yearnings fly away
in search of a South of passion and enchanting realms.

So many frowns have been raised, though, by these doubts of convention.

Eyebrows stern, delineating hardness in faces,
smiles withdrawn forever,
a pariah I have become by looking out these windows of containment.

Universes lay outside, waiting to be discovered,
loves so profound, romantic beyond all poets' reach,
while in this shape of body-limited,
my intentions orbit every cell and organ,
repeating a mantra of surrenderance,
awaiting a sign of acceptance.

Monarch butterflies fly back from their winter break,
erratically wobbling themselves north in dwindled numbers,
assaulted by human greed and insensitivity.

Yet, they flutter back in color, and reproduce with passion,
and subject their beauty to admiration and awe.

Fluffy, they fly
in such an absolute un-aerodynamic fashion
that even God wonders at his creation.

Thoughts come from dark spaces, behind curtains,
in off-Broadway stages.
They perform in flight and song and captivate your energies,
lead you to ruin or laughter, these rascal actors sublime,
engendered as they are by brewing instincts and impressions of yonder

when we wandered around in all shapes conceived in space.

They are mental butterflies that lead to the fields of consciousness
that populate the mind, harbingers of self-knowledge.

Awareness rushes through time,
like latitudinal monarch migrations
searching for warmth and life and love,
to express Beauty
in a clumsy flight of colors and random spontaneity.

All layers of spirit are aligned today
as cycles integrate one endless concert of moments.
Tranquility reclines on my back
as a soft pillow of time in clouds,
and I sigh in breaths of giving and appreciation.

LAHAR

The universe laughs
at all attempts to digitize moments in rigidity,
to construct havens of safety
in the middle of the constant change imperative.

Feelings, wavy as butterflies in migration,
bypass all engineers and mystical pundits,
making spontaneous mischief,
jumping over all formulas and prescriptions,
unlocking love torrents, inviting cosmic passions and dawns

to an infinite realization
that surpasses even creation and God together
in a love fulfillment of capriciousness.

1 LOVES 2

One
has no boundaries or limitations;
one is One.

The heartfelt Song most infinitively exquisite
is eternally swallowed in the boundlessness
of the Oneness.

Songs need a listener as much as a singer;
singing is an act of two.
But there is only One.

Expressing colors and preparing feasts of texture
in combinations unimagined
is the artist's dream.
But expressions of rainbows require the eye of the beholder,
as well as the dancing colors.

Art cannot be expressed within
the All-contained-in-One
boundless receptacle of One.
Art is an act of two.
But there is only One.

Love is the most subtle essence,
the substance of union,
the nature of the boundless One.
Love romances through the interplay
of longing and coming together.

But the All-in-One cannot long in separation
within its boundless eternal Union.
Love flows through the interplay of two,
the lover and the beloved.
But there is only One.

Two is the imagined possibility of One
to appreciate its boundlessness,
to hear the exquisite sound of the Song,
and to display and admire rainbows in color and form.
Two is the reflected image of One.
Many is the boundless creativity and imagination of One
as it loses itself in an infinite perfect game
of hide and seek,
so that every time One finds itself in the Many,
boundless joy resonates in infinite timeless light
of Love, Song and Color perfection.

One is the only One.
Two is its mirror to love;
many is its compassion to enable infinite moments
of appreciation and glory forever.

One and two and many are all One.

One loves two, and many, all the time.
I am two seeking the One in the many,
but also I am the One losing myself in the two
and in the many, to long and long,
and let love flow and be.

WALTZING MOLECULES MAKE THE HEADLINES

Molecules waltz in pairs.

They make their own music
which reverberates everywhere.

Their recombination dances are so creative and artistic,
each one of them generates new energies and beauty.

The dance of molecules is just magnificent.

Molecules waltz in pairs they are,
excellent partners and gregarious,

although it takes them an effort
not to go astray —

as they may when they become too wild.

Then they unfold and simplify,
the most daring releasing shouts of energy with great pain
while separating into elements and atoms —

simple stuff.

But when they combine in troupes
networking in web-like structures,
molecules then create their masterpieces:
those cells that taste and differentiate —
the receptors of color and aromas

and kisses. (Can you guess how many waltzing molecules
it takes to make one sublime kiss?)

They grow into complex formations of
organs and bodies and persons
which in turn generate
thoughts and memories, wars and loves

simultaneously in all time zones and altitudes.

It all lies beyond the headline news,
these secret organizations of miraculous societies
of dancing molecules
that serve the purpose of creation
by singing Beauty's contrasts.

Headlines are caught up with recording
the games of the silly,
the exchange of empty word formations,
trying to win the ratings competition,

for they ignore the origin of its constituents

of particles coalesced
out of that terrible terrorist explosion
set by the One without a Second
that wanted to use for a while

its imagination.

The first flights were frightfully accelerated and dark,
rushing out of the wound in the womb

that linked everything with its shadow.

They gyrated and head-banged and even pirouetted,
then condensed and cooled their heels

in atom-homes.

But some set up fires in the suns,
And then there was light —
and they saw each other

and they liked it.

The atoms came together and had you-know-what.
And many linked for life
in molecular arrangements that gave rise
to so many wild new forms

such as the mother-in-law.

And some arranged and rearranged

in trysts of every color
exploring the boundaries of being
and free love.

Zillions of waltzing molecules made
beauty and memories and time

but no headlines.

Till one glorious night of day
the molecular dances that enable every sigh
bloomed in the awe and humility

of an awakened soul.

The molecules combined one last time,
performing their last most sublime dance of light

TO MAKE THE HEADLINES OF THE UNIVERSE

AQUA VIVA

Liquidly it flows, through crevices unknown,
refreshing gutters, nourishing bucolic springs,
falling on thirst from heaven, flooding all surfaces and presence,
womb of oceanic life, sustainer of all cellular processes.

Aqua viva, sacred water of life:
it rains from the Ocean then evaporates and flies,
shaping clouds that look like you and me,
and ponies and snowmen.
Puffing cotton balls that absorb the humidity of the soul,
until so pregnant they cannot do any more than give birth to rivers,
and respond to the thirst of the land.

In gratitude, all flowers bloom,
and gardens become green, and misty mornings emerge
as mirages in the horizons, pink with the games being played
by evening clouds with beams of sun that enamor them
in a daily display of beauty supreme,
which most of us miss, as we play with ourselves.

Once fallen, it is imbibed by thirsty avid plants,
their arms, wet with dew, raised in praise,
their rooted feet cool, deep inside the ground,
wet with worms and interstitial rivulets
absorbing precious gifts of life so pure and magic,
to build the food chains that feed consciousness
at it evolves into Picassos and Mother Teresas,
Gandhis, and Hitlers and Attila the Huns —
the phantasmagoria of form
that in its infinite diversity enables the contrasted relationships
through which life experiences itself, and love in everything grows.

Every aspect, every clump of Earth is molded into form
through the process of Beauty;
all is required to cast the perfect tragicomedy
that leads to the Grand Finale of realization.

At that instant drops meet the Ocean,
merging into liquid infinity,
forgetting their gutter and spring moments,
and all other necessary gradients and pumping stations
that lay in the path from quenching thirst to drowning.

SACRED GEOMETRY

Lines are aspirations of distance and time,
growing out of an urge
original.

They intertwine in lattices and entanglements;
they fly in verticality and lie in bed embraced;
they bounce in space and kiss at crossroads
in Cartesian patterns.

Sometimes they crisscross at random, it seems;
other times their intersections are thought
by spiders.

But lines always meet,
perpendicularly or tangentially,
as the curvature of spherical space
mandates.

Every point of light that arises from the source
seeks another in darkness,
inevitably through all time and form,
in every possible arrangement.

Really, the Universe is a one-liner;
a word expanded in reflection of itself
that multiplies its ghost images of imagination
till eventually it tires of bouncing
and consolidates in simpler understandings,
arriving finally at
just one
point.

SONGS OF THE ANCIENT SEA

The Ocean is cascading.
As it falls, its thunder of silent being
enlivens all drop-forms.

Imagination is so imaginative
that its images live in Universes
vaporizing up from explosively silent Ocean falls.

Ocean blue, extending beyond perceived horizons,
flooded plains of yonder
fed with the torrential pouring
of tears of joy and pain
from life's eyes,
as it plays games of hide and seek with Existence.

Some drops have become so alienated by foamy bubbles,
that although being all water,
they believe they are separately dry.
They fail to see the tear channels
that link their misty flesh in drainage to the sea.

Misty, humid-like, enveloped in moments ethereal,
drop-selves are carried inevitably by currents and waves,
born in the turbulence of that original fall.

Our fingers of spirit, are wetted in the storm surge
of swirl- conceived light-years ago.

Rest, dear elements in vapors combined;
gracefully float, as the ebb and tide
defines your bubble-shape and direction.

Enjoy the ride to your Ocean-self.
Sometimes white water moments can be scary,
but then think of your lake moments.
They alternate, in the stream that takes you back to the Ocean,
without bubbles, without foam.

Ocean breathes in tides embracing all,
don't build any futile containment walls,
they will not last.

Stay in the shore, frolic in the wavelets that invite,
familiarize yourself with the water,
soak till you are ready to drown,
and lose the bubble that separates you from the water of life.

THE OCEAN IS MADE OF TEARS

One sunset by the Ocean immense
I realized that I had wept it all.
That it was alive like the water in my cells,
and pulsated in my blood flow.
I drowned then without remedy in its fathomless bosom.

I was reborn shortly afterwards in a shore remote,
with my bare feet washed by the surf.
It was morning and I did not know myself,
just this sense of being made me alive
as I sought to explain and understand.

All of a sudden everything was right;
there were no complaints, no claims, and no debts.
Everything was serene
as the sound of the waves around me.

I walked in awe. I bathed in light.
I marveled at my hands being part of me
like the sand and the stones and the passersby.

How can it be so simple — I thought —
so perfect, so ordained.
I laughed and cried at the same time
at the joy of being aware that I was not a drop,
that there was only Ocean.
As I walked endlessly in that state
I remembered unfolding gradually, being all.

I had walked for ages.

The kiss of the Ocean changed my life.
I came back to my fragmented perception of things,
but I never forgot the light
that surrounds everything in a continuum,
the serenity of Oneness.

I now seek it in the eyes of the other,
in the stars, in the tunnels,
in my nights and days,
in my despairs and joys-
hoping to drown again someday.

A HUNTING PARTY WE ARE

Absolutely together, as infinitesimal particles,
we hurled out of the stillness of Being,
searching the paradise of self-consciousness.

Bouncing on the boundaries of nothing,
we expanded space with our cosmic dance.

We held hands most intimately in our quantumness.

A hunting party we were, amongst numberless others,
sent out by Being to explore,
to arrive at the knowledge of Oneness.

Rebounding on each other,
we coalesced into forms more settled,
rearranging our possibilities
in more elaborate patterns of matter and energy.

We built more complex bodies
to experience qualities of essence,
like melting and flowing.

We were endlessly connected by most intimate nuclear forces.

We bonded in molecules so closely
that we reproduced and self-replicated,
becoming life that transformed light into flowers and aromas
through which the universe explored itself
in a garden of color and fragrance
in all possible states of vegetation.

We were together in those original puddles of life,
and the gardens that ensued.

Next we acquired locomotion
to explore all dimensions and niches,
from crawling underneath to flying in the heavens.

Walking together, our hunting party evolved and evolved
until we came to know that we were.

We bonded so close;
we ate each other, and mated,
struggled together against predators and hunted together our preys.

But now we see each other in recognition,
endowed with awareness, human.

However, sediments stirred-up with our searching
have deposited as inertial instincts.
All those volcanoes, novae, predation, the survival struggles,
they now combine as solid memories
etched on the mirror of our consciousness,
preventing us from seeing our true reflection.

The procession must continue as we clean our mirrors,
as we sift past records,
shaking them loose through alternating roles and gender,
through the enactment of so many different plays.

Our hunting party continues the search for knowing in human form.

The most first particle, born out of the divine womb,
after much ricocheting, tasting, struggle and love,

finally knew itself as really being the Ocean of Being.

Love was fulfilled with awareness.

Love and Infinity and the emerging never-ending bliss inundated all.
The Beloved was born out of this embracing of Infinity
and the yearning particle bouncing in space.

All were always endlessly connected to the Oneness unconscious impulse to know,
and now all were connected to the conscious knowing of Love.

Hunting parties now search for the Beloved,
knowing he has a face.

The Beloved, having been in the surge-to-be of yearning,
radiates pulses of Love as a Beacon in the night,
so all hunting parties can see the way back to the source.
Love can now infinitely rejoice
as each one of the innumerable particles
returns and recreates the forever bliss of knowing.

The procession progresses
through the many mansions reflected in the house of infinite mirrors.

Alert hounds now and then perceive the trail,
the fragrance of the Most Beautiful One.
And while learning the intricacies and subtleties of this romance,
they become aware of being endlessly connected as One.

Those eyes that now look with light into yours,
that compassion that moves you to heal and protect your fellow ones,
those nurturing hands that caress the fallen,

the bright sounds of laughter,
those smiles blooming like gardens in our faces
when we humbly recognize the uncertainty in each other.

It is all part of this Life budding, budding everywhere,
in a miraculous emergence of form and sensibility,
striving to become,
mandated by that most original Urge
to know the essence of Being: Love.

Can't you feel our hearts beating music,
our incompleteness being filled by love-flows
as we recognize our connections with each other
with our hunting party companions?

Now a time has come in which cables are laid everywhere,
like spider webs in the forest,
and images and symbols
traverse the space between us in a continuum of thought and electrons;
our planet is traveled fast by air,
bringing our bodies closer in time.

Our hunting parties are coming together.

Eyes are now seeing more eyes than ever before,
distant eyes of all colors and shapes
expressing the same yearning.

Beyond the bias of the reflections perceived by each of our limited mirrors,
we sense this.

We all sense a new dawn,
as the Beloved's latest beacon of light
beams through the connectivity scaffolding,.
simultaneously revealing in our hearts
that we are endlessly connected —

Because we know each other in Love

FRAGRANCE BOUND

Silently, this sacred secret spills.
in storm surge of evolution.

It floods every corner of mind,
body and heart, and makes limbs airy.

Thus we walk in depth outside, while sinking,
the air in words vibrating, like songbirds in seeking.

These skins wrapped around in forms possessed.

We move and intersect in glances and meadows.
Think in pairs and spread in multitudes,
this loneliness of many.

Together, we started this mirage of differentiation,
in one primordial flash of curiosity and whim.
To know how many One can be.

Sailors in matter-essence,
our particles bound with forces infinitesimal.
Growing in knowing, they complexified
in this lattice-congregate that
evolved until it reproduced.

Dancing all the way, my dear beloved ones.
To this music of curiosity and whim.

Today we find, as the wine spills in surge of secret and sacred.
We find each other consciously, even in the midst of denial.

Even as we cling to this phantasmagoria
of things possessed and possessing,

we know, we suspect, we intuit who we are,
and recognize the light beyond the original flash.

And we make noises in words,
and dance and make plans and wedding vows.
We do all the rites within,
contained deep in memories of have been there.
Our genes twirl and curl
as the currents from the silent surge
spill over the sacred again in our hearts,
and we find each other again.
And decide to walk hand in hand while time lasts.

Fragrance bound.

MAHAPRALAYA

Evening breezes have chilled the fire.
It ran away like a child scared of the shadows,
sinking into depths profound and remote to laughter,
where stillness and tiredness now reigned.

Galloping messengers were sent out to seek help.
Where have all the words gone that captured the essence,
where are now those heart visions and the transparent limbs
that crossed the walls of limitation
and sailed in poetry and imagination?

The outer limits of the universe had reached their balance
with the forces of nothing; they rebounded,
losing the expanding momentum,
and the architectural designs of the cosmos folded back.

A total collapse of worlds. Stars and galaxies
crashed on their centers as the chain reaction of return was triggered,
and everything conceived in space crumpled with a thunderous noise
that no one heard, as all normal sentience was deadened
into a point infinitesimal,
an atom so dense it made no sense;
and that point of nothing through which everything that was
had been imagined went back to the stillness that lies beyond conception.

Oneness rested again its tired essence
in the deep sleep of eternal contentment,
its curiosity reined in
— a pause of latency.
Romances were suspended, longing held in abeyance
when Being took a deep breath,
and inspired the conceived into its infinite serenity.

Evening breezes heralded the collapse of form
and the languidness of Being as the theater closed.
All the characters disappeared
in the sacred script of the Director.

Until the next season.

Nested in the love-to-be,
we all lay waiting as One for the next breathing out.

To continue our game of joy.

BLESSED ARE THOSE WHO HAVE NO PURPOSE

Palpitations drum deep inside.
There is an upturning of ancient crusts
— layered with so much passion —
unbeknown to the ubiquitous observer.

Yet they are witnessed by sentience, as a pain about to burst
on account of mysterious rhythms and cycles of Ocean:
the ebb and tide that takes you to the same place you have always been.

Life's purposes are like ephemeral pyrotechnics
shining dark in the zenith of our ignorance,
distracting our glance from Beauty.
That ever-present, non-locational Beauty that permeates all,
transparently traversing our bodies and ego-minds,
to become the continuity of the possible,
and express itself through our full moons.

That only One conscious Womb
engulfs all of our passing shows,
and rests our turmoil in maternal coos exquisite.

Shy away from any certainty born out of mind-games;
it will only make you believe that you are naked,
and make you fall into self-appreciation of your worth as a drop,
multicolored and witty — which you really are not.

You are the Ocean within and without,
the boundless Womb of Being supreme
that is forever protecting, creating,

destroying those surface bubbles of air,
that for a moment or two give illusory existence to separateness.

It's just the Infinite's game of ebb and tide,
to tickle itself and be everything it can imagine.

Brilliant night fireflies,
daughters of the cyclic mating of sunlight,
have been dormant for 700 years,
underground within the darkness of our soul.
We can sense them now, churning, buzzing, crawling,
preparing to emerge like cicadas in a hot summer.

They offer a way out from this flatland of purposes,
be them noble or ignominious, because, notwithstanding their nature,
they are the same lies that we tell each other
as we wait for the explosion of light inside:

That spark, not related to any interpretation
or ego point of view;

That free dance of fireflies in luminescence,
radiating joy, free of any purpose —
religious, patriotic, romantic, economic, whatever.

Just a reverie of pure joy
to illuminate these dark caves of mind that we have constructed
as a shelter for the tender palpitations of Being
as it enjoys its creativity, its Beauty, its infinite purposelessness.

Blessed are those who have no purpose, for they are in tune
with the Eternal Reality of Existence.

ALL DANCES ARE DANCING TONIGHT

All dances are dancing tonight
in rhythms exotic and elegant,
like swans in love on a moonless night.

Whirling in cadences of light and atom,
they unfurl like petals in storm and fall in the autumn
of quiet as the feet get tired of jumping around.

And what can be said
of this circumstance of being, this condition of human
enthralled by the awe of not knowing,
yet mischievously enjoying the tears
in the bouts of laughter and tinkling of bells
that happen no matter what?

Lovely, one would say, as we die.
But then, is there anything else to be done
than to ponder and suffer and smile?

Tonight all atoms are bursting in laughter
from fear of containment,
and spilling their musical notes in the vacuum of spaces
infinitesimal and intimate
like each point of departure of Being.

Everything rolls down these hills of contentment and misery
in mystery of delight, rumbling and bouncing
and merging in manners never described before.

Long, red vaporous dresses,
black suits with pointed black shoes and silver slippers
shuffle across the floor,
as stars ricochet and the earth trembles again
in creation-game mode, as we dance, dance, dance tonight in endless music

And forget all the things that we had to forget,
and forgive the forgiving of the unforgivable.
Smiling, we sing silly songs ephemeral, eternally as we dance,
dance in whirling motions ecstatic like the Universe.

THE BREW IS BITTERSWEET; THE TEARS

FERMENTATION IS A MALODOROUS PROCESS

Pain is rain that nourishes growth and full blooms.

Do not remain at ease in moments of seeming repose.
Enjoy, but be prepared, for these are intermediate landings
in the spiral stairs that take you to the heights.

Churning is the engine that mixes all together,
effacing any acquired pose,
any belief assumed so strongly
that one actually identifies as being it.

We lie beyond pretensions.
All piety and seriousness, all lustfulness and hedonism
all mysticism and innocence
run through us like scenes on a cinema screen.

They stay on the screen of our consciousness for a while,
as one journeys these winding roads
across these interminable landscapes of peoples and things,
as one play-acts the assigned role in the charade.

Fermentation is a bubbly malodorous process
that yields enchanting brews of joy.

Stop worrying about the intermediate stages
of whatever you are caught up with.
See them as steps envisioned by the master chemist
in his formulas for a supreme product of you.

Do not confuse yourself with transient phases,
nor become alarmed at the churning and seething.
As you come to a boil, everything will become clearer,
all those moments of doubt and pain will be transcended.

So carry on with your present sac of burdens and postures;
and keep an open hope that they too will go.
In recognizing that, you will carry them better.

Trust the master chemist: he knows the formula.
He is the one behind the churning;
he manages the ingredients and stirs them accordingly.

In the meantime,
smile
if you are in one of those intervals of kindhearted stillness and reflection.
And don't complain too loudly when the heat is compassionately applied
in your further synthesis.

Fermentation is a bubbly malodorous process
that yields enchanting brews of joy.
Just surrender to the master chemist.

TIMELESS TIMES

These are timeless times
those already gone,
the inevitable ones.

They gather like north winds
their cold fingers pierce the skin.
As lights in the distance twinkle
senselessly.

Timeless times
keep the rhythms of life.

They cause, distances to elongate
and memories to agglutinate.
Everything collapses into loneliness.
Sleeplessness is heralded,
and laughter hides in cold breezes.

This pain of time,
marked by strange sounds and lights.

A quiet nostalgia, like an evening dew
is perspired under cold bed sheets of yesterday.

Somewhere, beyond the noise,
hidden forests are denuded,
and unexpected barriers and borders melted.

My spirit just sits by the shore.
With the suspense of one who waits for centuries.
turning breath into sighs of maybe.

INNER PAIN

There is no pain like inner pain
when everything bounces hard
on the hermetic and impenetrable bubble
that encapsulates you.

When you enter the mood of brood
and remembrance.
When you are overwhelmed
and don't know what to do.

All escape routes blocked.

There you are, alone, absolutely alone,
no crutches to hang on
all the universes doing a mahapralaya on you.

It is a very untidy situation.

All of a sudden your latest desire doesn't matter,
the recent buzz word won't tickle you,
and the fortunes and antics of politicians,
patricians, and celebrities,
as well as those of Tom, Dick and Harry
cease to exist.

THIS DAY THAT NEVER WAS

This day cannot be.
It has not happened yet
No headlines or buzz for hype
No plans or theories to describe.

It has not been imagined.

So I rest within potentials
Under bed covers unexpressed
Till wake up time.

This hidden song stirs
Itching everything
Yearning for dreams

Exploding in consequence

Mother, your bow was too stretched
Now I am hurled into this space

Still embedded in the unimagined
But cast inevitably in panoramic
Illusion

Born out, yet at rest
Expressed, yet not

Wondering why,
inevitably as I lie.

SOMETIMES

Sometimes I weigh a planet or two
and cannot measure the circumference of my self
as it extends beyond boundaries never understood.

Sometimes I feel fragrances of coffee and roses
in the palms of my hands,
in a strange mélange of romance and morning papers,

I imagine myself in a Vienna cafe
my coat wet from snow,
my head filled with some new waltz dawn

Sometimes, I feel the hands of my mother
nursing my wounds in healing;
sometimes, I am a womanizer
liberating energies in wombs and almond eyes.

Sometimes, my smiles illuminate half the world
whenever they fall;
sometimes, my tears create floods that drown
my inertias, my planets, and my soul.

Sometimes only sometimes,
I see the delicately omnipotent invisible hands
that hold me all the time.

MARRYING THE GROSS AND THE SUBLIME

We speak in turns, and say what we must.
Negotiating each word of praise and complaint
Playing the games we trust.

We have become so many anyhow,
that there is no way of discerning our
point of departure.

In this rapture of living
we have just forgotten Being.

Oh well, it is meant after all,
part of the needed entertainment to Be.
So let's keep up pretending, this you, this me.

Rolling down the hills of least effort,
sometimes waking up to loss of comfort.

Not knowing, but pretending we do,
till sometimes an absolutely humble mood,
ambushes us in the backyard, as we walk.

Cell phone in hand, full of purpose and command,
we suddenly crumble and cry out — from the heart.

Every cloud laughs then in puffs, wind huffs in leaves,
and birds sing melodies of partnership,
of lovers seeking warmth
and company.

It is not an epiphany,
just this daily bread of frustration and enthusiasm,
combined in one stroke,
when life becomes both gross and sublime,
at the same time.

CONCRETENESS

Help me to be concrete,
for I can't bear the divine
Inundate with theory this mind,
fill it with new and obsolete.

Being is too painful to these eyes,
distract me with body ailments,
and lots of people passing by.
Fill the spaces with headlines and laments.

Help me do things concrete, like plans
outcomes, and models of life,
let everything be measurable in span
and achievement, for I can not bear this light

Please, invite me out to play, whatever game
it doesn't matter if there is joy or pain.
I just can't bear this unseen presence
It is so simple and stark naked in essence
So brother and sister, steer me back to the concrete,
the latest gossip, tragedy, strategic plan, or pleasure.
Take me out of this dereliction, ground my feet
For I just cannot bear this Being lacking measure.

Let there be noise, and headlines on war and flesh
weddings and reverie, talk shows and villains
and yes every day controls, with manuals that address,
how to live, repair your car, and make plans of plans.

Fear and security must go hand in hand to entertain
and provide the thrills that we all need to forget.

Let the lust for profit and success fuel the rest
so we are all caught up in this mess, and not wander in vain.

To that terrifying terrain of the divine
I pray in desperation please!
Steer me back to the concrete,
flood my body and my mind
For I cannot bear this naked being

I rather hide in I, you, me and mine.

CONTRADICTIONS

Voices in my dreams urged in contradiction
"remember the Beloved to forget everything,
forget everything so that you might remember him"

Heartaches gathered in a storm of wings
to ravage all the things that must pass.
Last few drops were falling, and filling
the glass up to the brim, to a point of spilling.

Nobody can sleep under this assault
— I said out loud — as I walked out of bed.
Wolf packs of pending were tearing my flesh
memories of perhaps-not-done-right sitting on my chest

Subtle forms of loves still budding and misunderstood
gyrated incessantly within, mind in brood.

— What else can I do — I said swallowing water to thirst,
mouth parched with words that would not come out,
feelings so long that they trampled in themselves,
pains here and there making every part of the skin taut.

Gasping for air in the anaerobic subtle sphere
muttering prayers in laughter and fear.
Knowing not again,
how to disengage from the falling debris
of my own deconstruction.

Down on my knees begging to be humble
Hoping to forget in order to remember
Hoping to remember in order to forget.

GHOSTS

Ancient stories surged from the vaporous mist
reflecting interactions now gone:
moments of love, laughter, sadness, joy,
lust, angst, anger, serenity
instants exchanged with so many,
all paraded on the screen of my consciousness,
-like movie reruns.

A mélange of forms old and new,
touchable and untouchable shells,
were smiling, dancing, provoking, irritating,
loving, imploring through a million eyes,
portable like mine.

Looking out from that same,
insubstantial primordial creative essence
that imagines all the images,
including the imagination of the imagined.

NINDA

Every word has become a sword
Everything is so wound up
Like threads left to their own
In a forgotten chest of drawers

All conversation is about the other's faults
Or sometimes about their virtues, in contrast of course.
All seems so distant from possible
and desires continue to bubble-up, secretly…
within those unreachable caverns behind the faces
that define each of these containers of petit-consciousness
these pockets of Being expressed in our personalities.

Looking and reading and judging and comparing ourselves
through these myopic lenses of eyes swollen
for lack of laughter, lack of feeling the magic of just being.

STILL CAN'T FIGURE IT OUT

It is no longer a question of happiness or satisfaction
it is just the remoteness from that shout inside.
These layers of guise between you and I
this business as usual of singing the everyday.

Imbibing in light all forms and shapes
and sound and taste, feeling alive,
yet somehow not being there at all.

Screened by panes in a house of mirrors
reflecting only skins and sensations.
Long gone relationships, appearing as in a screen,
projected solitary in two dimensions of color and profundity.

Three hundred trillion cells at unison
are exchanging ions, each in their task of sector.
All aggregated in one awareness of being
condensed, coalesced, in infinite bonds of
forgiveness.

It crosses through all of me and beyond,
this loneliness of many, this togetherness of none.
I tickle myself and laugh and weep and desire and meditate,
as I fail to comprehend this All that spawned me,
and became in me so unique
as this particular pain and joy, as this indifference in stillness.

NOT ENOUGH LONGING

I am wounded by concepts,
drawn to mystify and daydream.
Food is rotting in the drawers of my mind,
and nobody is picking up the mail stuff,
my muscles are losing their tone.

Debts are dancing gleefully
around the fire being set in my heart,
waiting to consume my roasted body
like a pig in carnival.

I have anointed my forehead with the symbols of hope,
I have breathed in and out,
I have closed my eyes and made deep sounds
that no Tibetan monk can emulate,

I have stood in circles with folded hands
praying at unison to the Oversoul.
I have danced in dervish, and pronounced incantations,
I have drafted memos and business plans
in logical frameworks of poetry unknown.

I have done the rituals of non-ritual,
the conventions and the non,
and yet I find myself intact,
distant from the point,
carrying this fraudulent id.

Looking for the formulas
that yield that nectar of light somehow.

This longing, mama mia,
this longing is not yet painful enough,
this pain, oh dear God, this pain is not deep enough,
this fed-upness not full enough.

DREAMS IN REVERSE

Memories are dreams in reverse.
They also have to be enjoyed.

I took a silent tour of rooms a long time gone,
savoring each holy moment revealed.

With the music playing in the background,

I paced softly as one does
when saying farewell to the dying dears.
I dreamed in memory and savored the beauty of nostalgia.

TASTING THE BREW; THE INEBRIATION

DESIGNATED DRIVER

I got drunk again,
and in this drunken state I cannot think too well,
so forgive me if I say something wild.

All these things are growing inside me,
like savage forests and impeachable thoughts.

I didn't know what to do;
all those roads crisscrossing my being:
highways, country roads — a lot of traffic out there.

I was lost.
I asked for directions,
but everyone seemed disoriented as well.
I studied a few maps to no avail;
they charted streets and roads
but had no northern star.

Everything was at a standstill,
for my confused, inebriated mind.
I sat and wept in fear, alone.

No one was there; they had all gone,
leaving me at those complex, multidimensional crossroads
without even a signpost.

I shouted from the bottom of my lungs this longing
for someone to give me the destination
among so many roads and paths
and instructions and diversions.

"What's going on?" I asked.
"Where is everybody? Where do these roads lead?
Which one should I take?
Please, dear God, I cannot drive this drunk.
I designate you as the driver."

Then said a voice resounding
like the thunder of church bells in a small town,
"There is no destination, there is nobody.
There is only you, my son, no-where — and even that is an exaggeration,
for you and I are not we but One, and there is no second.
Relax and laugh in joy; there is no time, there is no rush;
it is just Existence pure and simple."
"Wow," I said. "Wow."

OUR LAST GULP OF SPACE

The sun, as it explodes in thunder of radiation
emits caresses that melt as light
in the leaves of far-away plants.

Molecules receive them so tenderly and excitedly.
Gratefully they generate food and sustenance
for the genius of da Vinci
and the soul-singing of Francis of Assisi.

This violent tenderness of the sun-chlorophyll relationship
enables life and love.

Roofs protect you from the weather
but bar you also from caresses of galaxies.

Sometimes one needs to drink a few stars
to cure heart-loneliness.
Yes, sometimes a few scoops of star-sprinkled space
helps a lot to ease the pain of waiting.

So take the handle of Ursa Major,
use it as a ladle,
and help yourself to a drink or two.

Ah, the things that one can do
without that roof that delimits vision and mind.

Let us write a roofless book,
with transparent and wet pages,
sparkling still with tears and fallen stars
spilled over from our last gulp of space!

I CANNOT GO BACK TO THE CHEAP STUFF

Now that I have tasted your ruby wine, I cannot go back
with any gusto to the cheap stuff.

Oh, I do go back, driven by this pain, but I remain
completely unsatisfied.

Now that I have tasted your wine, my dear,
I yearn only for your kiss
of red vintage.

THIS PLANETARY CREATURE

Trepidation.

My legs have become roots,
sinking into the generative power of the Earth.
Amazed, I see leafy vines encircle my legs, my trunk,
asphyxiating me in a tight embrace of earthiness and life.
My mind shouts for help, as branches penetrate my ears
and pierce my brain,
squashing memories in liquid of time,
denuding concepts of form.

What's happening to me?
I was so airy with independent locomotion.
Now I am attached to the ground;
gravity is sitting on my shoulders.

My body roots imbibe nutrients
and sense the fire beneath the surface.
Volcanoes are raging in my guts,
continental drifts tearing me apart,
generating flows of magma and cataclysms.

Why? I was so happy to be light,
full of words so bright and spiritual.
Now I have become a central core of inner fire,
ready to light up again the Universe.
I am a man, metamorphosed into this planetary creature.
I need some rains, some heavy rains to soothe me,
to wash my arid mountain slopes and accumulate in overlapping oceans.

Clouds are gathering in the East, foreboding storms,
terrible soothing storms to fill up the placid lakes that lie in me,
and bubble up that fragile vulnerable being
that makes me swim and dance again,
to take your hand and help you cross
that little bridge that lies beyond
the sacred spot where all
are metamorphosed in secret.

AMBUSHED

All things outside congregated with a deafening tumult:
Clouds, entire forests, multicolored song birds,
monuments, stones and beetles,
an ocean or two, and several long rivers,

Mountains too and words, concepts, ancient books,
old men with long beards, children's smiles,
as well as bodies — so many bodies.

Hungry they came to see me, all things on Earth
and some stars.

I felt cornered by this ambush.

Shadows lurking in darkness
arrived also with their mysteries.

Everything was battle, preparation, desire.

The multitude of existents
rushed to my point of consciousness,
crushing thought and feeling.

I returned naked to the womb.

Serenity, shaped in suave hill formations
overtook the extremes of mind.
A gentle dawning light ensued,
a long restfulness of wayfarer kissed my forehead.

The curtains fell for an instant of forever.

All hands were purity of child.
All forms collapsed into myself.

Everything was again potential.

DANCE ON THE RIM

An old man said once:
"Sir if you don't want to fall into the well,
don't dance on the rim."

Merging ephemerally into one another,
dissolving in you this me;
Body-mind beating in just one heart
like a womb prisoner awaiting birth
into something else free and whole.

Covalently bound in chemistry and force,
prayer consumed in yearning,
intertwining legs, hopes, dreams and stories
in a moment of nowhere.

Eclipsing the nausea of every day's thorns and roses
beyond early definitions and proper smiles,

this impulse of flight carries me to fairylands
archetypally stored in ion migrations
of mitochondria and myth.

An inviting abyss of divide prompts a fall
into a well so deep it has no depth — surface only.

Yes, let's dance, dance, dance on the rim

to see if mercy, that together star,
dissolves all hope and makes us slip
into the profound beyond all dreams;

To forever drown in the one drop
that is Ocean and naught,
that is word and stem
of that Being beyond,
becoming to be.

A METASTASIS OF MOON

Last night I placed the moon between my eyes;
thin veils of grayish gauzy-clouded materials surrounded her so gently.

She dissolved gradually into my brain
like a sweetmeat in a hungry mouth.
My neurons glowed in moonlight soft,
processing impulses in a more romantic and reflective way.

Signaling to faraway operational stations
was now moon-mellowed.
Image receptors in optic nerves were interpreted in tones of bluish
texture,
and passersby glowed in an eerie otherworldliness.

There was a sense of tropical breeze, of sandy beaches,
of songs of forest in the midst of the pavement
when the moon lozenge dissolved
in my scratchy brain last evening.

Word games, interpretations, and knowledge
had been assaulting me all day long.
How many words are there in languages?
What are the things that they describe?
I wondered, as I drove under the influence
of a moon-drunk brain.

A hundred-mile-long line of words,
like elephants catching their tails in procession,
are contained in the recesses of my mind.

A million times more are stored on the bookshelves of libraries
and forgotten attics, packaged in neat bundles of black and white,
waiting to be brought to life, legend, and conviction
by the gazing beams of light from somebody's eyes.

They are classified into things measured and predicted — science;
things measurable, predictable and controlled — technology;
thoughts about whence and whither — philosophy.

Each one subcategorized.

Then there are manuals of all sorts:
for cooking, business and sex,
for etiquette and car repair,
for every thing conceived in space.

There are books about the inner worlds non-measurable,
books of symbols.
Those which try to chart the subtle, the ineffable;
metaphysical explanations in mythological rhymes,
which use the stars and the planes of consciousness
in a woozy poetic language,
to describe your placement in the cosmos,
allowing for each a casting and a role
that is understandably enchanting.

It is really a beautiful story
that helps counterbalance the arid word chains
of the describers and measurers
who fill the bookshelves
with life's procedures and prevailing norms.

There are also short lived endless word chains
describing the last tragedies and gossip in repetition,
to saturate your mind and the curious nature of the human condition.

Books, titles, words, definitions
embraced with so much passion and conviction.

It is like grasping clouds with desperate hands
to feed a hungry child,
a thing so unsubstantial and impossibly futile,
while creating the illusion of nourishment.

I do not know much beyond this body sac
and its accompanying consciousness.

What else to say?

Oh, yes. I have been under the influence
of many of these books of different types and inclinations
and have matriculated myself in many a school of thought
that meant so much to so many at any one particular moment in time.

But nowadays with this moon tumor in my brain
— I can't explain why —
I have become word shy.

The neurons seem to have become engorged and fluffy,
hypnotized into a trance,
and cannot handle long sentences

Now, this is very embarrassing,
as people do write me and phone me and even stop me on the road
to talk and say anything.

I look at their bluish contoured figures
while listening to their vibrating voices
that reveal secrets behind their word chain addiction;

I react to all these communications,
avoiding the long definitions,
the logic which escapes my understanding,
and just feel the undertones,
which are somehow quite clear
for my moon-infested brain cells.
And I answer in kind
with a moon response.

TEN THOUSAND EYES

Ten thousand eyes became my own anew
as I unfurled my arms in an embrace to see.

My heart exposed,
laughing incessantly
as the Ocean within, spilled.

I heard words pronounced,
flying like killer bees.

Thoughts dawned in rhythms of sound;
mounds of sand and sea emerged
behind curtains of uncertainty.

Birds of light were flying infinitesimally
as my brain defined things perceived
and my loins urged continuity.

White puffs in cloud and smoke
were mixing on stage.

Exciting theorems woven in fear, not knowing,
they tap-stepped in marches of thousands and one,
collapsing eventually in breasts of women desired.

This painful joy of bliss.

This trembling for you, my dear mischievous one
who dared to become while already being.

Aghast, I am shackled and freed by you,
caressed and crushed
by those destiny-loving hands so suave
that you have.

Myths and stories and atoms and bonds
coalesce all into this sham
to give, to laugh

as the madman shouts in the plaza,
his hands in frenzied gestures
repeating angles forlorn
while stars gazed down from infinity.

Embraces and sinew,
minstrels and mistresses
all parting lips.

Open books in biography,
telegraphy, technology and poetry.

All words, bullets displacing nothing,
bouncing in echoes of sameness,
reverberating, regurgitating themselves
in noises of being, while seeing...

But knowing not.

Crashing, imploding, exhausting
into this beating of a heart so powerfully lovely
that it has imagined itself clearly,
unconsciously,
in the middle of nowhere,
of nothing, of night.

Ten thousand eyes becoming my own
as I unfurl my arms in space
in an open embrace to see

Me.

COSMIC NEST

The Universe is nesting in me,
incubating some creature of joy.
Its intrusion pushes my inner walls to their limit.
How many novae can you fit in one frail male body
unaccustomed to nurturing womb protocols?

All this dark matter, intergalactic spaces,
billions of galaxies with countless stars and dreams
are bursting within.

How did it happen?
I was just walking as usual, avoiding the extremes;
I breathed in and the Universe contracted,
surreptitiously slipping into my entrails.

Now, I feel moonlight glowing in my eyes
and suns burning in my loins like a satyr in heat.
Electron beams and photons of light flow through my bloodstream
to the interstices of my tissues,
and I radiate an aura of cosmic rays
that scare away the surrounding people.

This pulsating, expanding universe
has lodged itself in the womb of my heart
and is pumping blood-light that shines
through my pores like a body-planetarium.

Whole planets are bouncing like marbles
in the congested spaces of my body,
its gases and liquids spilling and mixing with my inner fluids.

My brain is full of creativity and possibility,
uncertainty and direction.

The Universe is nesting in me,

lacerating my organs, confusing my body sense.
I don't know anymore if I am inside the Universe
or the Universe is inside me.

I weep in Oceans and love in magmas.
I fear in supernovae and black holes,
and my sense of humor is inundated and made possible
by the immense tickling effect of neutrinos
as they run amok under my skin.

I open my mouth to explain myself
to this friend who thought I was acting weird —
and out came these violent beautiful swirls of galaxy.

He ran away in disarray.

Had it not been for those blessed neutrinos
I would have retracted to a black hole of shame and night-ness.
Instead, I laughed and laughed at my imagination
about the Universe nesting in me
in such a silence that I did not know and had to imagine it all.

Then the Beloved whispered:
"But the Universe is truly nested in you,
incubating the joy of consciousness supreme."

THERE SEEMS TO BE A WILD UNIVERSE

There seems to be a wild Universe
unfolding everywhere and inside
with molecules unbridled
and hidden passions of lonesome lover.

Even little things like neutrinos and quarks
bark at the sole mention of control
by these egos of ours so tender.
I don't even want to tell you what is said by the big things,

like suns, galaxies and hearts.

THIS JOY OF TODAY

Every atom in my body, every thought occult
within the recesses of my mind,
every secret longing stored
within the golden coffers of my heart
has come outside today to see the dawn.

They are all dancing, hands up in the air,
their subtle forms and bodies sinuously following rhythms
unheard before in time.

This joy of today, like the one of tomorrow
and the one from yesterday,
draws its substance from the never-ending,
from the never-beginning simplicity of that ancient stream,
pouring out from the heart of hearts pierced by the whimsical curiosity

to know the limitlessness
of its capacity to love.

A NON–SUICIDAL TERRORIST EXPLOSION

Fireworks are mere supreme shadows
of the original big-bang show,
when out of mischief,
One decided to explore and to know.

Generating all this love,
this attraction, this loveliness of Being,
enhanced only by its shadow masterpiece
— the contrast of duality.

My passion, dear,
is a volcano that would consume both of us
in ardent eruptions and flowing lava.
I have to devour the whole Universe to satisfy this hunger,
and you are in the middle.

I lie serene in a postmortem of desire
— that fire that leads the search —
and I wonder at the next wave,
while I contemplate the horizonless savannas of my mind at rest.

Please forgive me, dear, for my intensity.
It is born of that non-suicidal terrorist big-bang explosion
that took place eons ago.
It was so hot and blazing then
that it etched my memory with these impressions,
and I am still in embers.

ROOM OF ENDEARMENT

Reclining against those walls,
I listened to ancient songs and words so simple.
Birds calling through rustic windows
rode the breezes inside of enchanted forests and countryside.

Time was evolving in galaxies serene,
as love stories unfolded supreme,
and tears rolled down cheeks of maidens and young men
in conversations with the one who interpreted Silence.

The room was absolute, smiles genuine as roses.
The presence was so certain that there could be no poses,
no words — just divinity in elegance of authenticity,
a sense of belonging nowhere else,
of being home on a Sunday morning.

Mind now drifts at its best to memories of those sublime moments;
the rest is just paraphernalia.

I lay my back against those walls of eternity
as I listened to the story of the Universe in a room like no other.

Since then I have wandered around,
opening doors in comparison,
trying to match that grace.
All lies in a lower plane of turmoil and praise,
of I, me, and mine in all colors and shades.

In my mind at its best, in friendship with my heart,
I go back across that threshold of carpeted truthfulness
to the assembly of the witnesses of the Most Beautiful's last sighting.

I find a corner, a soft cushion, and forget myself
as I sink into rhythms of honesty, purity, humor and light
so bright, so wonderful and unique that they just do not exist,
except in that sacred realm of love given, in total abandonment
and surrender.

SUN HUNGER

Transparently falling looking for a substance
that is not yet formed.

Density has always aggravated me.
It defines you in space
as a shape from where your consciousness peeks out,
shyly, always in doubt of its extension and continuity.

I searched this morning for some information that would tell me
when the sun was going to fall upon me and liquefy me into light
so that I may cavort again freely
and ricochet in the stars, to help those who read,
to bounce on phosphorescent screens of women and men in love,
who seek each others' spirit through electronic pulses
in tune with their heartbeats.

Within, somewhere beyond colors and sounds of thought,
lies a Silence that rests, while playing in bliss,
a Silence that finds itself forever in the illusory noise of its own voice,
whenever the sun falls upon the density that separates, defines and
enables Oneness.

FAITHFUL DOGS OF PREY

One of these days, the sun will fall upon me
and flash my all.

Incandescently, I will burn as a morning star
and light up the shadows of myself
that always remain around me like faithful dogs of prey.

Then I will see.

THE FORECAST HAS TO BE ENDURED

I am surrounded by these self-created walls.
Sometimes I climb the roof to breathe
but always come back to sleep inside.

I aim to overcome, through bridges and space travel,
resolutions and grinding of teeth — a supplicant also I have become.

Still, the forecast has to be endured,
the seasons will turn, and the sun just does not fall.

Spiders weave a web of capture that define their own boundaries.
Mind is elusive, clever, witty, and obsessed with its own sets.
Mindsets: they juggle words, add logic, a pinch of feeling,
and remain satisfied with their scrabble solitaire.

But not me.

WHEN LIFE WAS AN OPEN FIELD

Those rolling hills in sunset,
dotted with golden-lit dwellings like hobbit villages.
Elysian Fields in purplish hues of gold.

I remember those corners where the breeze
would be so mild and fresh
that it would caress you like an embrace of God.

I remember mornings of gifts and joy when you opened surprises,
innocent enchantment everywhere
before definitions wrapped the sweets so tightly,
when life was an open field to explore.

THE INTERROGATION THAT EXPLODES WITHIN

Machines bursting in sound and purpose
are mitigated by tender hand caresses.

Symbolic Information in digits of quantity
cannot grasp the beauty of your sinuous smile
or the delightful light shining round through your eyes,
or the surface of your endless skin of grace.

This beauty of contrast
with voices remote and kisses so deep
escapes rulers, scripts, and engineers themselves
in the joy-and-pain madness to bliss.

The sinews of body-mind,
the caverns of thought
and concept,
collapse and effervesce
as we wake up to the magic of awareness
and recover awe and possibility,

as we negate the objectivity of ignorance
that leads us to linearly define
that which lies beyond explanation:

Like the rose, the birds, the planets
and that interrogation that explodes
constantly within you and me.

NO ONE KNOWS

Wounded in bliss, footfalls accumulate
and leaves fall on grounds unknown.

Seeds are unfolding latency,
reaching out into self.

Nothing.

Rosebuds opening in gardens of mirage
standing in awe at their own fragrance.

Present in presence all are
membranes exploding, interfaces of light and tissue
waking and walking in universes of joy
still hidden.

Forbidden little children's games
unwinding, accumulating playbacks of sounds
unheard and primordial
built-in throughout the structure of the nothing
that reveals Love.

This pulsation is inside every realm,
inside every conscious second
recognizing recognition.

Symbols are just songs, embraces
emerging in oneness, pretending
a manyness of possibility and colors.

Glyphs, letters, words, harmony
are continuously pouring through all.

One moment during this rain,
somehow remembrance knows,
and bows and merges,

flourishing in embraces so profound
that no one knows.

No one knows.

ONE HUNDRED THOUSAND ROSES

I have one hundred thousand roses
to counteract each word of cynicism.

They are not mine; I stole them last night from the Ocean
while moonlight slept.

I was drowning for awhile
in a sea of voices
bleeding wounded stories.

The transparency of mental spaces was
stained by the blood-light of dreams torn
by the knives of derision.

The flood of Light-blood
carried me to the estuaries of my heart
feeling lost, empty,
dismembered.

As I spilled my soul
into the ocean,
She opened in infinite embraces
of white-rose gardens.

Under cover of an incurable moonless night,
hidden in the inseparability,
I prowled the gardens
and stole the white roses.

I filled my saddle bags with
petal munitions
and emerged to defend

the sweetest stories of Silence,
our dreams, the new.

Beware now, be forewarned:
I have one hundred thousand roses
to counter each word of cynicism
and un-love.

They are not mine; they were stolen from the Ocean last night
while the moon slept.

THREADS OF LIGHT

This ocean-wet music
paints green rolling hills inside,
I see them upon walking the path
towards any destination.

Unhurriedly.

An unknown disquiet stirs within
as I spill in inevitable rhythms,
day by day, like rain

I flow in torrents and rivulets.

Far away sounds of hometown nostalgia,
are concealed behind the walls of my soul.
In spite of the apparent tranquility
of my smiles to others

My consciousness is fruit-flavored,
my fingertips explode in flowers and thorns,
when I stretch my arms towards essence

This damp music of Ocean, bores through me
like warrior spears' and artists' imagination
I melt in multicolored waxes
conforming forms in dance,
born in water rhythms,
that take me to undefined seasons.

Beyond cold winter and spring blooms,
the melancholy of autumn, or the passion of summer

Unusual seasons, fragranced by people awake,
moonlighted by moons in simultaneous phases,

My hands form a chalice, supplicating,
My eyelids palpitate in nervous flutters

Yet my heart is serene,
like the sacred ground of Andean plateaus,
Filled with blood it overflows through million glances,
and searches for the dazzling sun that shines,
in that place where there are no days or nights,
because shadows are the threads of light.

LOSS OF INNOCENCE

Tapestries of simple smiles.
How can innocence be restored?

Dark eyes shining without fear
revealing the universe and its spheres.

Sparkling eyes of child
What happened in between?
What corners conspired against dreams?

Today I waiver all procedures and rest
In a sort of twilight.

My temples are breezy,
my thoughts distracted with foam and song

I feel I belong to arms so suave and long
that embrace my soul in reminiscence
of an innocence now gone.

STONE PALACES OF FOREVER LOVE

I recline
on stone palaces of forever love,
Everything reclines in soul
as the every morning miracle of things comes on stage.
Frozen in a total instant,
consciousness is not even aware of itself.

Drifting like remote autumn leaf,
paralyzed in endless motion.
Unfolding in absolute changelessness,
sensing the potential of potentials.
Somewhere never ending films are being projected
Portraying all possibilities, dreaming all dreams,
achieving all realizations
within the womb of expression,
in an embryonic whim

Nothing forms as I recline, in this point beyond now
Eyes passively perceive light,
like hollow bones capture wind in the desert.

Nothing to say, or dream, or illustrate,
everything lies prostrate within
Bundled up in a moment which has not yet been
waiting for the unseen.

SHIRT POCKET

I am ready to fold my world
And place it in my shirt pocket
I am sorry folks as you all
are going to be crumpled
close to my heart.

But I am ready to fold my life
to keep on walking.

ADIOS

All blue has spilled now
the skin is open and raw
Everything is scorched
it has been a long day of forever

There is happiness of funerals
and a sadness of weddings.
A sensation of lost and found
at the same moment of time
Spaceless horizons
crowding my chest.

Sitting by the shores of myself
I write in my diary of child
"Today without knowing why
I started with elegance and love
the final march to the Ocean"

I am heading Home

Beginning to hang these clothes that have kept me warm,
defining and allowing so many loving encounters.

To all I bid farewell and ask forgiveness
for any confusion and missteps

Today, I feel the vast loneliness, woven by so many,
waiting for me in smiles of absolute.

THIS JOY OF PURE BEING

Beyond the high speeds of the imaginary particles we describe
and much further than the field of infinite potentiality of the new verse,
there lies a most shy, omnipotent, innocent and inexplicable joy.

Let's make believe, like little girls playing at serving invisible tea
we are hearing this music unheard, and dance, just dance

Bring along the so-called sins and other deviations to spice up the rhythm
as well as the virtues and credits you can spare.

Let's dare to be absolutely naked in this purity so insane
that it can only be seen in moments of silence and then forgotten,
like sacred oaths unspoken

Pour the cups of non-existing tea and share with each other this instant
our little girl hands so poised and elegant as they serve,
the inebriating nothing tea that lies hidden,
in the shyness of the original explosion

Beyond the accelerated particles of our imagination, way in there,
impossibly near , hiding behind what has never been lost.
Collapsing in intervals so fine you can call them divine
yet it is all beyond words and languages, this one song

This joy of pure being.

ANY TIME IS A NEW YEAR

The seconds, minutes, and days of our lives,
are reflections reflected in mirrors.
Everything is a sea of energy waves
converging, resonating, distorting.

At the end only melted light remains,
beyond that, the tenderness of a child,
a simple caress.

The hand of mother in her goodbye bed,
the last embrace of a friend,
the tender moments shared.

One yearns, longs and venerates them,
through every story and tradition,
with memory and occasion.

Each day upon waking
each night upon day's review.
When you walk alone silently
in the surround of nature
in repose of body and mind,
in those moments of just being.

We yearn and long for, we venerate
ancient songs.
as a love that has long gone
but which is always there.

Every story, is the breeze that we see,
the faces that wake up to others in smiles,
or marvel in awe at the unexpected and quotidian.

Every explosion and tear
is but a preamble of new horizons,
of metamorphosis, of transformation.

Therefore every moment elapsed, every love lived
every embrace of friend stored within the heart,
every memory, every unbearable pain, is nothing but,
a point of departure,
a blooming of new fruit,
a dawn of opportunity,
a celebration of a New Year.

THIS INEFFABLE FEELING OF INEXPLICABLE JOY

This ineffable feeling of inexplicable joy
seeps in through inner doors so secret.

Hidden alcoves are opened on occasion, unwarranted.
No special mantras needed, or efforts in prayer,

oh well it can coincide, if you do that all the time,
that the doors open, as if a password was said,
but in reality it was just grace.
Flowing to you without conditions, like true love,
warming everything in a glow sublime.

Hearts melt down then and smiles flourish in stern faces,
bodies acquire a special rhythm, that prompts embraces.

Suddenly, the magic of Antares and the her legions of sister stars,
appears in the dark of night, like a princess dressed for her wedding.

What prompts that corner breeze to whirlwind of all sudden inside?
What can command the spontaneity of the divine?

No strains, no mantras, no discipline, no austerities, no wealth,
no prayer, no chants, no potions, no secret scrolls.
No formulas can take you there,
where the sun rises in miniature so bright
that its cool incandescence outshines daylight

This laughter of spirit is provocative and free,
one can only jump in the air if the body is still fit,

or sport a brightness in the eyes or a tenderness of skin,
to caress whomever comes across as it springs.

It is merry, happy, sublime, just perfect, this rhyme
is the engine that moves everything, the summa cum of love.
Yes that little candle, that swift breeze, that primordial song
which is found sometimes, somehow, somewhere
so unexpectedly inside of you and me

So let's dance to it
keep it in our memories, icons and traditions,
till one day, suddenly and in total serendipity
we again bow down
in that secret alcove of spontaneous combustion.
Our hearts on fire, our feet tap dancing the only song
that can never be predicted or asked for, or bought forth.
Let's savor the kiss of the Beloved
as it catches us unaware, and makes us be.
It is an old story, a romance of spontaneity,
which love only can see.
No coercion is possible, no bribery enabled, no route, no discipline
nothing can harness this whimsical graciousness,
that makes everything such a delight.

The flavors of the Beloved once-in-a-while- kisses are intoxicating
and you really never know when they will be in your lips.

So may the grace fall upon you one of these days again
so you may remember never to forget
that ineffable feeling of inexplicable joy.

TIME MACHINE

Moments of yearning and longing
cannot be ignored,
not even in the highest flights of fancy
of our escapist imagination.

Today, like yesterday, is already gone,
Tomorrow, like today, will be done
The only thing that will remain
is the shared moment,
the love etched in the heart.

That which we always, yearn and long for,
and venerate, that, which does not pass.

Today, like yesterday and tomorrow,
let us celebrate, arms up in the air,
our conscious shared passage through life.

Let us welcome with love
the present day, the days bygone,
as well as the hereafter time to come.

THE BOMBAY TRAFFIC COP

I fell, like a giant in an anthill.
The whole body of a Bombay traffic policeman,
flat on the street.
There was sound of laughter, at the falling thunder,
and blaring horns, catcalls, and whistles,
as well as the ruminant sounds of the Bombay
I remembered an era ago.

They all burst out in fireworks of mockery divine.

The ants were biting pieces of me,
every cell gulped with each bite,
the skin became open
like the doors of a temple wide.

Yet, I laughed rambunctiously, like the rest,
and found my heart out in the opening of my chest.

I was being devoured, by a billion creatures of hunger.
without even knowing their number,
but yes, they all conspired in synergy,
and chewed.

My scarce hair was taken for a joke,
my bones were split apart,
and the sweet marrow of my osso bucco shared,
like a delicacy fair,
amongst those cannibals,
that feasted on my bare body
without hope.

Tomorrow — I sang — as digestion started
of one of my parts,

In the future — I uttered — between the clamor
of my inner laughter, and that of the crowd.
Mañana, — I said — as ants disappeared my body
amongst shouts of joyful pain.

"I will be a belly dancer
in the bellies of these billion ones
that have made small morsels
of my dignity and self-esteem".

These vicious varmints have effaced my ego,
into the holiness of boundary-less,
I thought, as the last breath of mind
escaped to become insect tissue, earth,
molecules of naught.

In spite of the pitiful digestion,
and the burps of so many,
I was still present in a state non-descript,
and all heart corners were active and fit.

My soul became awake,
like a flower at night, when the moon rains.
All the pain and the laughter subsided
as one field,
and I entered the realm of child,
seeing all through awe and wonder.

I returned in a formless form,
whistle in hand, baton in hip,

white shirt washed out, in the light of yonder,
my insignia shining like the sun.

I returned to my post,
hands outstretched to continue my mission,
still unheard, unseen, un-minded, blamed for all.
I returned to the intersection,
with more passion than ever before.

Because somebody had to,
and because hearts can do no more.

NAKED NAKEDNESS

Nakedness reveals nooks and corners where stars nest.
Hearts then must be careful with the winds of words,
otherwise they will be like sharp swords,
wounding inadvertently the soul exposed,
creating terrible pains.

This is why we all, like tortoises, carry this weight,
in armature of skin and callousness of thought.

Sometimes, if we come too close to the naked ones,
those homeless, that love has made dispossessed of skin,
then our own carcasses and shells peel and fall
— as a kind of acute leprosy befalls.

We are then exposed to wind and dust,
denuded of pose, with no games to play anymore.
Our eyes fixed on glowing objects like moons,
our hearts surrounded by songs,
bathed in everyone's blood.

We want to die, even though we are already gone.
Relationships are no longer in the realms,
of I and you, and me and mine.

Those homeless lepers of entrails revealed,
have now become our peers, our life companions
our dreams.

Together we form choirs to sing inevitably
as we gather around the scorching fire,

that melts the skins even further,
that burns disguises beyond recognition
leaving not even scarred tissue.

Just that joyful emptiness of hopelessness,
that true nakedness, that even God is afraid of.

Imagine dressing up again in our pretense cloaks
to feign prudish smiles and frown in coquetry,
as we return to propriety,
after coming from those savage lands,
as we enter these sheltered buildings
we have imagined as real.

Imagine the difficulty of dressing up again in our pretense cloaks,
to feign prudish smiles and frown in coquetry,
as we return to propriety,
after coming from those savage lands,
How do we enter these sheltered buildings
we have imagined as real?

A WISE MAN ANSWERS

All multicolored bubbles thin as they spin
with Earth's turns.

Slowly, horizons are drawn, in suspense of remembrance
and the beauty of contrasting contrasts of nothing,
crumbles in precipitates of essence.

Deep thoughts and monumental creations,
universes portraying astuteness, elegance and lust,
disassemble like demolished buildings.
Clouds of dust bearing witness that they never had been.

But what is left of the distillate of that liqueur transubstantiated
that remains in the invisible still of that generative zero?

Was all that effort of nothing unnecessary to attain
that everything imagined and transparent.
that comes and goes unrepentant through these
people urns?

Where do the feelings of the distilled vapor fractions go,
where do the wisdoms learned sediment
the intuitions? the thoughts of could have been?

That amalgam that constantly drains through limbs
hearts and minds as life's rains?

Where is the rust, the mold, the debris of essence,
and to what avail so many stories and so much awe?

Moved in his heart a wise man replied

"to dream my son
because One has to dream, otherwise existence would be eternally boring-to Being."

"This is why in every individual brewing there is singularity. Diversity is the diversion of what always was and will be. So the illusion of nothing, sustains the reality of everything."

SONG BIRD

Today a song bird fell in my heart.
Stubbornly wounded, he sang and sang
I played deaf as always, so busy…
with this and that thing of mind

Running after a desire cherished
or in the inertia of fear,
burying my head in the sand.

Today, music erupted quietly, like a buffered volcano
but instead of lighting up incandescently all surroundings,
seamlessly in tranquility, it migrated to remote capillaries,
to interstices of tissues previously unknown to my blood.

All my issues and fervors were aligned in simplicity,
passion was focused in remembrance of love
and imagination was loose and pure, rejoicing in itself.

Today, as I opened once more the eye-windows to light
a song bird fell into my heart and sang and sang…

FISSION

Light-hurt, eyes bewildered,
an eerie awe percolating, like coffee
in the morning.

Atoms have split open
like bubbles of nothing.

Their entrails radiate energy,
vibrancy.
All sounds are now humming,
like machines in sleepless nights.

Little thoughts are desperately running,
like homeless children out of sight.

Fumbling, trembling fingers are praying,
prayers disapproved by rite,
inconsolably and
profoundly.

Tearing the ears of the God-head
-afraid for their lives.

Marching trumpets, sounds galore,
in the quiet night,
as atoms spill their beings,
of space and little things
in the realm of the broken heart.

That laughter, dear, of bells and carillons,
invitingly invites to what?

As we wander in this fright of just me
in this lonely dark.

Surely stars are shining their ancient time
of light.
Pouring the obscurity with loveliness of universe
seductive.

The moon, that yellow-eye of mystery,
is oozing magic and romance,
awaiting for a glance.
As we all lie preoccupied with labyrinths
of sinews and mind.

Life swiftly transforms mosaics,
assembling all intimacies
into multitudes unknown
to themselves.

Lightning has struck in kiss,
and split open all atoms of the heart.
From their entrails light is shining,
illuminating bloody chambers
reflecting lights
like in a discotheque.

This prison of geometry and ego
is avoiding the magic eye of the moon, at all costs,
so not to be awakened,
from the self-hypnosis of mind.

Frightened, running intermittently
through this market complex of
form and thought.

Evolving this sight of moons.
Intimately!
Infinitely!
Evolving from this i to the I
Inevitably

INTIMACY

There are secrets so secret, they have no contents contained.
Intimacy so deep it never surfaces.
We are wading floods within, far from everything,
smiles and proprieties don't reach those places.

Hidden sparkles in eyes might sometimes connect.
But not words, not pleasantries, nor greetings studied in pose.
Just those subterranean eye-lights that reside in the caverns of soul,
alongside the hidden knives that slice the other, out of fear.

There, where all the noises of voices are drowned,
where intentions are raw,
like cold embers in lonely nights.

Inside, bubbling demons and angels we all brew.
Alternating expressions, they manifest in faces and moods.
But they are just tips of hidden icebergs, hidden agendas
we tend to ignore.

In the silence of our nights we know more.

So, brother and sister let us remember
those secret places we all share:
our angel-winged demons, our mischievous angels,
and forgive each other constantly, permanently, endlessly.

THE MAN IN BLACK

Center stage, a man in black danced
conducting an orchestra of searching,
and people were transfixed in that present.

The music of his words created a symphony unheard.
It went beyond meaning, beyond words,
inviting everyone to an embrace, of grace.
Unbeknown by speaker or listeners.
it bubbled up from wells of being
and upheld everyone in safe harbors.

The performance of the man in black,
who intertwined ancient and modern,
distracted all somehow for a moment.

The noises of crowded bars and plazas subdued
as soloist and spectators were moved
by a symphony unheard that upwelled
from the bottom of the One heart in everyone.

For a moment or two everything was calm,
an embrace of Mother prevailed and soothed.
Forgetting and forgiving was made possible again,
in that infinite rest of soul, in that embrace
of grace.

ZENITH

I hurriedly walked alongside, trying to match his graceful gait flowing through garden spaces like enamored comets in nights of Brahma. It was so sunny and bright and I was so happy, because with the Beloved again in the garden, I need not think much about the flowers, they were all blooming for him.

I asked about something or other, we had an intimate family talk about this one and that one, and about my plans and not. Then in Silence golden, his hand in mine, he looked at me gazing from his eyes of mountain ponds and said. 'I have a question for you'.

I was delighted but anxious to be correct in my answer. He continued — what is most beautiful to you, more splendorous, sunset or sunrise?' I did not know at first hand what to say, but I concluded — sunset — without knowing why.

Good he said, good answer, and I smiled content. Now — he continued — but is it not the same sun? Yes, I managed to say to his rhetorical question. Have you noticed — that people only look at the sun in adoration during sunrise or sunset? — he added. Yes I replied.

But do people look at the sun at midday when it is at the Zenith? — he continued — No — he answered himself — people feel its warmth and enjoy its life-giving brightness, but nobody glorifies the Sun at its Zenith.

He walked pensively, it was time for him to move on to another house, to feed another heart with presence. 'My dear',— he said as parting words —, 'It is the same with the Beloved, people appreciate him in the past of morning and anticipate him in the advent of sunset, yet nobody acknowledges him at the Zenith of his presence, they all feel his warmth and enjoy the inner light of love that dispels the darkness of separation, and look for his light reflected in minor celestial bodies and artificial neon signs, but very few my son appreciate His presence at the Zenith of his manifestation.

I remained blinded and knew why...

UNWINDING ENTANGLEMENTS

So many voices whispering, shouting explanations.
Pundits with demanding frowns assassinating smiles.
Our eyes clouded with tears, not knowing why.

Sultry springs of dawn are about to explode
in a subdued laughter that grows.
As one comes to know, after ages of trying to unwind,
the entanglements that define our fears and our hopes,
to know that we are so absolutely naked,
like that emperor with no clothes.

Then our laughter dries up all tears, all anxiety, all illusions
we pick up our bundles, still yarned up all around
and start whistling a song of joy
to charm up our brothers and sisters as they walk beside,
each with their own baggage, each searching.

For that timeless laughter
that breaks the spell of one versus the other
For that time of endless joy!

JUST BEING THERE

Eyes open again
stealthily seeping in horizons,
sketching silhouettes of mountains
once seen captured in gouaches.

Suavely, dreams disperse,
like wing fluttering of transparent
butterflies

Through them, one could see ancient landscapes,
accumulated as a result of so much looking out,
through the windows of so many trains.

That twilight between the solid and the ethereal
glanced out, barely crossing the veils.
Yielding the secret subtle fragrance
of unexpressed awe.

The ground was covered by a humbled sky,
that ventured into low foggy clouds,
with rarefied gauzes as open arms,
and drops of time filling its humid misty vessels.

Barely whispering, lips murmured,
and temples, feverish with enchantment, trembled,
as diminutive garden buds narrated stories of old.
Walking us anew through paths drawn
in half opened realms, like cocoons about
to give birth.

The velvety texture could be felt,
in this new morning of horizons,
gliding through the tranquil beauty.

Of just being there.

WHIRLWINDS OF SMALL THINGS

Consciousness stretches and spills
through the cracks of mind.

A whirlwind of small things,
of the most insignificant moments,
accumulated like dust in the corners
of an unkempt room, appears.

I watch them like one who sees
ants crossing the ground,
with a buffered awe
indifferent to detail and analysis.

My heart beats as always; unbeknown.
and body lies integrated in its identity.
Thoughts walk around slowly, in a mist,
indecisive of staying, tired of being desires.
Like friends in a wake.

Where is this new aftertaste taking me?
This new aroma of ancient carnivals?
This sand in my toes?

The footfall takes me through thick forests
and abandoned closets.
From this vantage point I try, to try anew.
I seek but without enthusiasm
I dream but in black and white.

Yet, there are wind chimes everywhere
and today was better than yesterday.
About tomorrow I cannot even say "who knows",
because I do — tomorrow will be again the same.

Yes, morning bells ring to glory
and birds sing within.
Every time that I feel, surrounding me,
these whirlwinds of memories
of small things.

HELP IS ON THE WAY

Healing voices of silence gallop towards me,
as I drown in the uncertainty again.
My arms are embracing myself, with arms
so long that they forgot their shoulders.

Music-in all tones and hues.
is turning on
choruses forlorn.
Abandoned ships in ports
are becoming alive with cellos and violins.

My eyes open to see the gardens of nowhere
to behold the roses blooming
to feel alive once more in the middle of it all.

BEYOND QUIETUDE

An inevitable quietude threatens everything today.
Movement rests, all motion is laying down.
Sound has frozen into silence.
A presence of serenity invades all.

Thoughts are perched in mind's branches.
Tranquil, devoid of energy or desire
they sleep a deep siesta.

Feelings have collapsed into one point of consciousness.
Hatreds and loves, pains and joys are intimately embraced.
Duality is in suspension, exhausted, resolved, spent.
Experience no longer determined by opposites.

Existence is now an endless calm of moments,
a time without time, the undefined no longer yearns
for explanation.

Words are now like munitions without war,
stored in useless piles, devoid of sentences.

Serenity has rained on the universe
images have folded into a point of
light to be.

Today waters are like before they were;
a stillness in lake.
Today caresses and kisses are naked
in the purity of love

Everything is quiet, tranquil, a windless shoreless sea.
Being is fulfilled without motion, trajectory or destination.

My soul has disappeared in itself,
it is not alone, nor accompanied.

Today time and imagination rest without space.
Beyond dreams, beyond the possible and the impossible,
In this point of Nothing that could always Be,
in this intelligence supreme.

IF SLEEPLESSNESS WAS WEALTH,

If sleeplessness was wealth,
I would live in a palace alongside the moon.
From my window I would see the gracious spilling of light
over everything that crawls and flies.

A sidereal breeze would herald mornings,
sprinkling stars on my window sill
with music so delightful, that smiles
would spring in lovers lips and dreams.

I would walk all night awake
while everyone else is asleep.
Imagining ways to dare, to let go.
So that those impulses of forever
dissolve the tribal context of my mind
-the spaces of my ignorance.

I would dance with the svelte night,
so elegantly dressed in her dark cloak,
adorned with sounds of mystery,
and stories of love, shadows and memories.

Tender rains would then pour on me;
maternal woos, sensual lips,
and the laughter of children in eternal play.
— a total feminine display.

My body would collapse.
All the jars within my mind would pop open their lids,

spilling silly things like intellectual pride,
irony, sarcasm, wittiness, and cynicism.

All that insistence in showing off
would vanish like vapor
through the windows of the mind-heart open ajar.

If sleeplessness was wealth, everything would have been forgiven,
Laughter would fill every instant and bitterness would be a flavor
in a British drink.

SONGS OF LIGHT; THE BELOVED

MELTING

Love knew neither boundaries nor limitations.

It poured.

All birds came out gaily from the nests in my heart
and melted like snowflakes in memories of sunlight
so profound that they will shine forever in the continuum
that links us as One.

IMPERCEPTIBLE

This presence imperceptible elongates its arms
in an impossible embrace.

No one ever sees the flow of this river,
healing, nourishing with balms unseen.

Everything melts upon its contact:
words, thoughts and poses.

Exhausted, all folds of form live.

THIS COSTUME HAS BEEN A GIFT

This ragged disguise that clothes my assigned role
belongs to you, Beloved.

You are the soul writer,
who has scripted every possibility of Being,
every potential of your infinite cast of characters,
as they project from your imagination
to display the Beauty of creativity and the spontaneity of Love.

This saga of your self within each is an epic poem,
an aspiration sublime, a romance without limits,
unfolding every moment of imagined time,
in every dimension of conceived space,
like a flower offering to the Beauty of infinite existence
which incomprehensibly Is,
and which intuitively we feel in our hearts

when Silence dawns within.

The interplay of your fictional characters,
as they evolve the subtle plots
you imagine in your unbounded spontaneity,
crisscrosses the encapsulated fields of mind
and hides the voice of your Silence,
as you play this hide-and-seek game through all,
for the sake of the joy of finding.

Soul writer, as I stretch my legs today in a moment of quietude,
and savor the joy of glimpsing your invisibility once more
— upholding all —

What can I say to you that you do not know?
What symbols can I rearrange in a sequence that you have not anticipated?
What songs containing melodies, that you have not already sung?

I wonder.

As I sit naked now, on this bundled disguise I have been calling me
— the role that you entrusted in this never-ending play —
looking out through the windows of my soul,
marveling at the overpowering simplicity of your cosmic womb,

I have come to know that this is a sacred role,
that this costume is a gift of the most fine embroidery.
So dressing up for my part, renewed,
I bow down to you, Beloved,
and stand up and walk to the horizons of infinite possibility.

Grateful that you have given me the chance to be your vantage point
from this perspective of perception,
so you can look at yourself from every angle
to glorify the infinity of Love

POETRY OF THE NEXT DISPENSATION

How can I tell you?
It is an embrace so overwhelming
that it takes away all preconceived notions.

All words undressed of meaning;
sit down useless by the road,
waiting for content.

All masks are removed
in that moment beyond conception and imagination.

There, one stands absolutely naked
even light stays away, too shy.

The simplicity absolute of the Beloved's kiss,
his arms open in welcome, for eons lost.

There is an understanding
that goes beyond any knowledge;
it lingers as the forever origin of most sublime music,
that first and only note.

How can I tell you?

There is a secret I want to share,
the most sacred secret in the Universe,
but I cannot say it, or write about it,
for this secret can only be felt at the core of your heart.
A secret not yet revealed.

My role is simply to wait,
and hold your hand while we sing,
make sure we don't bump into anything
as we stumble out of the encounter with the Most Lovely.

He is always there unseen
but now wants to show us his newest disguise,
the one used in the last masquerade,
when he seduced us silently.

When he set in motion the poetry of the next dispensation,
renewing his eternal vows
of love so intensely
that ages of sediments melted in our eyes,
and our hearing was enabled.
In our hearts a little window opened
to see Beyond
all those posters we had put against walls,
all those images of passing that we did not want to let go.

He loved so much, the Most Lovely,
whose past is remembered and worshiped,
whose present is ignored and forgotten,
and whose future advent is anticipated with great fervor
and longing.

NO KID'S GLOVE

No words, no maps, no explanations
no mantras or soothing balms
to heal the blessed labor
that forebodes the birth of joy
and the death of pleasure.

No measure, no rules, no paths, on the edge
of this devastating sword.
No kid's glove in the hand that bears the hunters knife,
that will de-carcass our heart from the expected
and throw us back into the deepest dark of night.

So we can see the light rising, eclipsing all.
In that interminable apparition of dawn
that shines from the Beloved's smile.

A SIMPLE MAN PLAYS CHECKERS

An old man playing checkers
does not speak;
avenues are silent within.

The new dispensation was wrought
in Silence.

Orchestras will convene to sing the primordial song
echoing again deep within all

thanks to this visiting Love
again escaped from the scaffolding
of formulas and propositions, systems and derivations.

A quiet, simple man plays checkers
with an open heart.

Concerts will stem from this deep
simplicity of soul;
not the words,
not the sounds,
not the charts —

just that profound recognition that surges within
and lightens the eyes
before thought and mind, before theories of reconstruction
or definitions of the impossible divine.

A simple old man quietly plays checkers.
And his eyes
and his all
say out loud in a voice unheard,

"Real things are always given and received in Silence."

THAT BEAUTIFUL ONE

That beautiful One, with hands of roses and eyes of everyone,
walks the Earth every so often.

To confirm the romance divine,
to kiss life with the wisdom of Existence,

She/He loves and suffers conditioning
to light the candles of our souls.

We meet, again and again,
and our hearts recognize those eyes whenever they see,
and that smile that takes the breath away.

MINEFIELDS OF MY OWN CREATION

Forgetfulness came with mind,
so full of thought.,
All my being then clamored for you;
in the loneliness of emptiness
I missed your tender caresses.

Only vacant eyes like mine reflected back,
speaking all sorts of inanity,
nothing that would quench a drunkard's thirst.

Confusion grew in void mental spaces
as heart struggled to surface once again
to embrace you.

Suddenly the printed image of your eyes of light
burned my forehead
and penetrated memories archetypal.
I recognized you somehow
when I saw your face captured two dimensionally.

My body shivered;
ancient rocks displaced themselves in deepest molten magmas.
I rediscovered lost continents.

Unknown silent memories
projected themselves onto the screen of my consciousness
like shadows of light.
And I knew, my Beloved,
that it was you again in a new disguise of eyes.

Ever since then I walk on your footsteps
as you help me tread safe ground among
the minefields of my own creation.

At times I think I know,
and venture a step out of synch with yours,
and I fall in pain, only to look up from my fear
and see you with a lucid smile
urging me to hurry back to your outstretched hand.

YOU ALONE EXIST

Now. After the presence, what is left of the ordinary walking about?

Everything is flooded with yearning, and this nostalgia clutches my breath.
There is no longer any fun in breathing, or anything else.

Silent and remote are the star dances.
Memories are sharp knives slicing the bygones that defined me.
I am all alone in your absence, which is everything.

My hands are perfumed with your touch.
My eyes are hurting with your precious images,
My touch forebodes being in dimensions of whole.

Here, under stars forlorn,
something within, pains unknowingly.
It grows out of dark silent tunnels
in caverns within abysses.

This longing to recline on your body,
and look at horizons, as dusk falls.
These deaf songs thudding inside my veins,
swallowed by themselves, before music comes.

This numbness everlasting
pounding in abandoned temples.

Aching, in soft tones,
unable to justify, not even compassion.
This smile not revealing
the inner turmoil that ravages my soul.

You alone exist.

This nothing shadow that reflects your infinite expression
prays to be absorbed in the presence that is all.

As you alone exist,
what is then this part of you,
that feels the absence of your presence,
and feeds this longing to be?

HALT THIS MASQUERADE

This carnival has been going on for so long now.
Could you put a halt to this masquerade
and reveal yourself to me in your naked beauty,
that I might know your all, and laugh in the joy of eternity?

It is late, my dear, and we have been here for such a long time
that I am beginning to forget
why we ever got on this merry-go-round.

NO, LOVE IS NOT EASY

There are those who talk about happiness like a commodity
that you can buy in a corner store,
A thing that comes out of exercise, will, and a mantra,
or two.

Which can be grasped in method and sold like a brew.

They don't know

There are those who talk about pain as if it was a botheration
another of those stains you can wash out of your clothes
with strong soap and determination

A mental thing that you have to overcome,
a sort of psychological poison for which they can serve
the antidote.

They talk about a simple formula
to overcome pain and release joy.

I wonder if they have ever fallen in love.
For love is a terrible pain of joy
It is a wound that does not heal
and makes you whine and makes you sing
at the same time.

Love is not easy, all lovers, know that path of thorns.
Drunkards they are hovering by the Tavern
hoping the wine will flow.

Their whole being just focused on the Beloved,
all else is just a passing show that entertains

Now for a while of course you can live in that limbo
and be amused by concepts of happiness
and quick things to soothe your simple botherations
That, which you call pain, those ego-irritations

You still have to discover the pain of separation
The joy-pain of true love that never ceases until
you are not.

So for the moment in the cage remain sage and
etch your smiley's on the wall to scare away
Those irritations that you are calling pain,
It is okay.

But stay away from being a lover,
for that pain-joy has no boundaries
No rest stations

It will keep you awake all night and day
howling your separation
it will keep you awake figuring ways
of how to heighten your adoration.

The light generated by this love will outshine
constellations of close up novas and suns
yet the fire will ignite your entrails.
The pain-joy of disappearing will efface you.

The wound of love is beyond the realm of easy
The lover's plight is no delight it is plain crazy

Avoid this madness by all means, refrain from exposing.
For once you are wounded you will forever fall,
and no amount of counseling or little books
or special corners and sacred nooks will save you.

Only the consummation of the moth compares
You will burn around the light of love until you die
and in that dying lies the secret of pain and pleasure
"love entails pain—the pain of the pangs
the thirst of separation, while constantly burning."

The great poet Hafiz said "O Boy! Pour the wine!
Then pour it again: At first love seemed easy,
but then came the pain."

So stay away please from Love street, if you want safe.
And don't confuse the proclaimed happiness-light
or the pain you can console with a formula smile.
With the joy-pain of the lover fallen, whose heart
has been pierced by the deadliest of arrows.

To him the sun rising is of no consequence
It is just a kind of illuminated darkness
He lives and dies only
for the light of his beloved's eyes.

A TRAIN WHISTLES

I prostrate myself,
and fall at the feet
of the infinite creativity
that surrounds everything.

A rhythm plays hearts,
as life evolves in form and content.
I just sit here on this corner and ponder,
in gratitude and wonder,
at all the faces that populate the envelope
that contains me,
like signposts of past and future.

Their voices oozing cadences of sacred.

The surfaces of their skin shining,
the glances of their eyes beaming,
their stories weaving, a tapestry of context,
writing the books of soul and paper.

Generating culture
inspiration, agendas.

I corner further in my corner
in fetal defense bundled.
My heart beating as an open wound
totally exposed to me and you.

Instincts brew
the dances that move the senses.

But at night crossroads appear,
and thin rain falls like tears,
of a love lost, somewhere.

A train whistles piercing the fog
making me sit amongst crowds unknown,
in a noisy quietude.
Then I remember all, trying to remember you.

SUDDENLY YOU COME

Today sadness floods water
and fields weep green

Mistiness collapses like mountains
within my journeying soul

A stillness remains as if nothing ever had been

My eyes are filled with sleepless eyes
opened in all directions yet veiled
Intensifying this torrent of mind

Then you suddenly come and invade all
And I surrender…

SOMETIMES IT HURTS, MY LOVE

Sometimes it hurts, my dear.

Endearment is so long now
that it crosses every boundary without papers,
lingers on porches and gardens of yesterday,
soars into space like an aimless moon bird.

What is there new in this world
that you and I have not talked about, my dear?
In this age-long conversation of fossil hearts and burning stars,
of eyes so deep, of tales in the middle of the night,
of sighs for ocean and fires of secret?

What is left behind, my dear?
This silence? This constant beauty and burden of form,
this multiplicity of points of view
that engenders so many aspects
and diversities and congestion?

Headaches rain like inverted springs,
and serious faces look sternly into the madness
that you have set into my otherwise normal self.

Aren't you ashamed of exposing me so?

Yes, I know it is your dream and mine,
but I am so attached to these onyric, insubstantial selves of ours
that I pain inside somewhere,
as I interact with my unknown others
and witness your invisible presence inspiring all.

It is becoming a wild thing to follow,
this creativity of yours, these games of solitude supreme.

Oh yes, deep inside I trust and have faith somehow,
that it will be rectified upon awakening,
and I do not doubt the beauty of your setting
and the infinitely beyond-Oscar-award quality
of your scriptwriting extraordinaire.

But sometimes it hurts, my love.

MORNING PRAYER

I will just have some coffee, love.
I cannot bear this self-imposed separation;
let's talk it over during breakfast, darling —
this never-ending story — and see where it takes us,
how this day's petals unfold,
till we meet again
under the covers in the darkness tonight.
I hope that one day you stop being so shy and secretive
and reveal to me your full nakedness,
so I am blinded by the flash of transcendental light
and fall asleep, fully awake within you, forever as One.

This is my morning prayer.

Lightning Source UK Ltd.
Milton Keynes UK
10 April 2011

170695UK00001B/7/P